ANATOMY
of a Trend

HENRIK VEJLGAARD

McGRAW-HILL

*New York   Chicago   San Francisco   Lisbon   London
Madrid   Mexico City   Milan   New Delhi   San Juan
Seoul   Singapore   Sydney   Toronto*

1 2 3 4 5 6 7 8 9 0   DOC/DOC   0 9 8 7

ISBN-13: 978-0-07-148870-9
ISBN-10: 0-07-148870-7

Library of Congress Cataloging-in-Publication Data

Vejlgaard, Henrik.
  Anatomy of a trend / by Henrik Vejlgaard.
    p. cm.
  ISBN 0-07-148870-7 (alk. paper)
  1. Popular culture. 2. Social change. 3. Style (Philosophy)
  4. Fads. I. Title.

  HM621.V45 2008
  306.09182'1—dc22   2007019120

To the memory of my father

Contents

Introduction

From Intuition to Knowledge

Many people have been led to believe that trends are about intuition. This is because the majority of the people who work with trends find it difficult to explain *why* something will happen the way they say it will. The explanation often boils down to "because I think so." Some people do seem to be able to predict what will happen based on their own intuition. Unfortunately, there are too many cases in which people's intuition has obviously been mistaken for us to accept the intuitive method. Furthermore, intuition is a skill that can't be learned by the rest of us. So because intuition is so highly uncertain, we need other methods if we want to understand trends. This book represents an alternative analytical method based on trend sociology.

Anatomy of a Trend analyzes a variety of trends, all of which have eventually become a part of mainstream society. This book isn't an update on new and emerging trends. Instead, it reveals the patterns behind trends and what we can learn by examining trends systematically. Such study is possible because there are predictable patterns in every trend. Most of the trends discussed in this book go back several decades. There are two reasons for this.

First, using older examples enables us to document that some of the patterns evolved over a long period of time and that they are well established and unlikely to change any time soon. And second, as we will see in the following chapters, trends take a while to emerge and evolve, which means that some time has to pass before we can finally conclude that what we are dealing with actually was or is a trend.

This book demonstrates that some patterns occur repeatedly whenever a new trend emerges. Although the world is changing all the time and this flux may eventually affect the patterns behind the trend process, these patterns are deeply rooted in human behavior, which also tends to follow fairly predictable patterns. Unless society is dramatically transformed and becomes radically different from the way it is now, the patterns that have emerged in the decades leading up to the twenty-first century are likely to continue for the foreseeable future. If such a transformation does happen, it is likely that the trend process will change—along with everything else.

Each of this book's seven chapters ends with a summary of certain characteristics that can be used to understand emerging trends. By investigating the people who have started trends in the past, where trends frequently start, how trends emerge and grow, and why trends happen, we can define some rules for spotting trends.

The purpose of *Anatomy of a Trend* is to give you tools that will help you spot emerging trends and/or evaluate critically and independently something that is presented as a new trend. After reading the book, you will be able to judge for yourself whether the latest "new and exciting trend" is a real trend or just a fad.

Trends are a unique and intriguing process of change, and they affect most of us. By following the evidence that is scattered throughout this book, you can get to know the intricacies of the remarkable social dynamic that causes trends to spread. We all fit into the trend process and play a part when style and taste are changing, but some may find that they play a bigger part than they think.

1

AN UNSOLVED MYSTERY

INVESTIGATING THE TREND PROCESS

In 1983, chefs were not using cranberries, an original American fruit, in salads and other dishes. But at the beginning of the twenty-first century, cranberries were used in food all over the world. Who made that happen?

Also in the early 1980s, hardly anyone had heard of rap music. But by the beginning of the twenty-first century, it had grown into a major music genre that could be heard all over the world, in many languages. What happened during that 25-year time period?

In 1997, only people whose style was considered conservative were wearing trench coats. Ten years later, trench coats had become fashionable in large cities all over the world. Where did this revival of the trench coat begin?

At the start of the twenty-first century, car manufacturers were introducing cars with a "retro style," inspired by car models from past decades. When did the interest in retro style start?

These questions reflect one of the mysteries of modern culture: how changes in style and taste come about. At a certain point, we can see that there have been changes, but how these changes come about is often perceived as an unexplainable phenomenon. It is, of course, the unexplored "gray area" of trends that we are dealing with.

With newspapers, magazines, and just about every other medium using the word *trend* on a regular basis, we are all talking about trends more and more—in both our private and our professional conversations. But for something that has become so popular in our language, we seem to know very little about what a trend is, how to define it, and how it affects us as individuals, as businesses, and as a society.

Most people can indicate what the word is referring to—something new or "hot." Often people will also point out that a trend is something "airy" or "mysterious," or something that is "completely unpredictable." However, this is, in fact, not the case.

When people talk about trends, most of them want to know certain information: What is the latest thing? What is hot or cool? What is the new style? What is the new trend in, for instance, home furnishings? Is the new style glamorous or minimalist? This book will *not* answer these questions. Instead, its purpose is to share the story of a trend and ultimately enable *you* to find the answers to these or similar questions.

By using the conclusions in this book, you will learn how to identify emerging trends, how to understand them, and how to make predictions concerning the course of a trend.

If a trend is indeed like a story, then this book is like a detective story; it will lead us through a plot where questions will be asked—and answered. Though many people are familiar with the meaning of the word, what is actually going on as the trend progresses is still something of a riddle to most people. With good reason: the progress of a trend is one of the unsolved mysteries of present-day social life. What is known is that the plot starts with one or more persons who create something new, in one way or another. The main plot, however, revolves around quite a varied group of people, the trendsetters. They are the central characters in this story. Without the trendsetters, there would be no climax and no conclusion to the story.

We know that the trendsetters set off the action and affect all the other characters in the story, but the intricate relations by which they make this happen have not been told before.

Anatomy of a Trend will delve into a lot of evidence of their influence. In keeping with the metaphor of the detective story, we will visit real settings and meet real people who have made a huge difference in our styles of living. This is very much a real-life detective story, with concrete answers to who, where, when—and why. With the full body of evidence, we will be able to reveal the anatomy of not just one trend, but all trends.

THE EVOLUTION OF A WORD

To truly understand this story of a trend, it's meaningful to know the backstory—the word's history. The word *trend* and the concept it describes are certainly not new. But for much of the twentieth century, the word was used only in very limited circles, mainly among statisticians and economists. In the last third of the twentieth century, it also became common in the fashion industry. And it is mostly via the fashion industry that the word *trend* and the interest in trends have become part of our everyday life when we talk about design and style. (The terms *design* and *style* are often used synonymously, but in this book *design* refers to individual designed objects, whereas *style* describes a certain mix of designed objects—for instance, designed objects can be mixed into a romantic style or a minimalist style.)

Originally *trend* was an Old English word meaning "to turn." This is probably why the word became popular among statisticians and economists. In statistics, *trend* means the direction of a curve. Often a statistician will use the word *trend* when the direction of a curve is not all that evident. For instance, if there is only a slight change in the curve, a careful statistician will talk of a positive or negative trend in the curve instead of saying that the curve is going up or going down (either direction can be positive or negative, depending on what the curve is representing).

When a statistician speaks of a trend, there is very little doubt that we are dealing with factual data. For instance, take the book *It's Getting Better All the Time*, where Stephen Moore and Julian L. Simon present the "100 Greatest Trends of the Last 100 Years," using official statistics to document the many changes that have taken place in the United States in the twentieth century. The authors provide 21 timelines in areas ranging from health to transportation to wealth to document what they see as improvements in all areas over long periods of time. Here are some of the statistics mentioned in *It's Getting Better All the Time*:

- In 1900, the average workweek in the United States (and in many other countries) was 60 hours. People often worked on Saturdays or worked five 12-hour days. By 1909, the average workweek had dropped to 51 hours, and by 1950, it was about 40 hours. The 40-hour workweek is still pretty much the standard for people who work full-time.
- As a result, workers have more leisure time today. The authors quote the work done by sociologist John Robinson, who has discovered that the average American gained about five extra hours of free time a week during the 20-year period from 1965 to 1985. Many factors contributed to this pattern, such as the number of vacation days, which more than doubled between 1960 and 2000 in the United States.

To a historian, these statistics are meaningful trends, but to someone in the fashion industry or a trend sociologist, they are not trends at all. They are nothing more than statistical documentation of historical changes. To a trend sociologist, a trend is not something that *has* happened, but rather a *prediction* of something that is *going to* happen in a certain way—specifically, something that will be accepted by the average person. Someone who is working with or interested in design and style will also use the word *trend* to focus on the very first signs of change, such as a sudden interest in ornamentation on women's clothing or consumers being attracted to a new type of car.

Clearly, a trend means different things to different people. But many people associate the word *trend* with design and style. This makes sense because one of the first magazine uses of the word dates back to 1936 when the Design and Industries Association in England published a magazine with the name *Trend* that featured articles about new products and new design.

People who are interested in or who work with trends can use the word in different ways. In popular magazines, we see headlines like "New Furniture Trends." In this case, *trend* means product news. Someone who is working in design can talk about the trend in the new car collections from the big car manufacturers. This will be a reflection on the product development that is going on in the car industry, so in this case *trend* will mean product development. Finally, a trend sociologist will talk about a trend moving from the trendsetters to mainstream. In this case, *trend* refers to a process of change.

Interestingly enough, these three uses of the word are interconnected. You can say that a trend is a *process of change* that (sometimes) comes about because of *product development* that (sometimes) results in *new products*. Which definition you use depends upon which portion of this flow you are focusing on.

Journalists, for example, focus on the first definition, product news, because *news* is what they write about. *Time* magazine, for instance, has featured a "Trends" column, defined as "a sampler of the latest in fashion, cocktails, technology and travel." This is also the understanding of the word that most consumers have.

The second definition, product development, is used in many industries, from fashion to book publishing. It refers to the product development that goes on in the trendsetting companies.

These companies create something new, and many other companies then copy these new products or get inspiration from them.

The third definition refers to a process of change that begins with trendsetters and moves into the mainstream; eventually this change may even fall out of favor. With this usage, if something is a trend, we are very early in this process—we are focusing on the very first sign (or signs) of change.

The focus of this book is on this third definition and how this process takes place—in other words, the story of the trend. Trendsetters play a crucial role in this process, as we'll discover as we delve into the story. The term *trendsetter*, obviously derived from the word *trend*, entered the language much later—in the first half of the 1960s. Both historically and today, the word *trendsetter* is mostly used in relation to design and style.

But trends are not limited to design and style; they also affect what we eat and drink, what we like to read, the movies we want to watch, and the other areas where we use the word *taste* to describe what we like. For instance, we say "My taste in food" (not "My style in food"). Therefore this detective story follows changes in both style and taste, as well as the behavior surrounding style and taste. It can, for instance, be about *what* we eat (such as Mexican food), or it can be about *where*, *how*, and *when* we eat it (e.g., in the form of takeout). But in order not to be too repetitive, most of the time I will refer only to style, even though this will often mean "style and taste."

CHANGES IN STYLE AND TASTE

Style and taste really undergo two types of changes; one of these is short term, while the other is long term. In the case of the style associated with Jacqueline Kennedy Onassis, we have an example of both. Jacqueline Kennedy, the former U.S. First Lady, was a style icon for most of her adult life, not just in the United States, but throughout a large part of the world. When Jacqueline Kennedy was First Lady in the early 1960s, her clothing style was the epitome of 1960s style. In the beginning of the twenty-first century, Jackie Kennedy style again became popular, but only among a very small group of people and only for a very short time. The comeback of the Jackie Kennedy style is a typical example of a short-term fashion fad.

The evolution of this particular short-term fashion fad began in February 2001 when the John F. Kennedy Library in Boston announced that on the occasion of the fortieth anniversary of Jacqueline Kennedy's emergence as America's First Lady, in order to explore her enduring global influence on style, there would be a special exhibition of the original clothing and accessories she wore at state events in the United States and abroad, all of which had been donated to the library after her death in 1994. The exhibition opened at the Metropolitan Museum of Art in New York City and went on to the Corcoran Gallery of Art in Washington, D.C., in the summer of 2001 and included a book on her style.

Behind the scenes, the Jackie Kennedy style was promoted to the fashion industry as "the next big thing" by *Textile View* magazine, one of the world's leading trade magazines for the fashion industry. So, just what effect did this show have on the world of fashion? Well, the style attracted the interest of some people in the fashion world, but it never really caught on in any lasting way. It was quickly forgotten. The following is a chronology of what happened "behind the scenes":

- In the autumn 2001 edition of *Textile View* magazine, there was a detailed article about the Jackie Kennedy style.
- In the autumn of 2002, the Louis Vuitton collection for spring/summer 2003 was presented to the press and the store buyers on the catwalk in Paris. The fashions were clearly inspired by Jackie Kennedy's style.

- In autumn 2002, *Textile View* again featured an article about the modern interpretation of the Kennedy style for autumn/winter 2003/2004.

- In the autumn of 2002 the exhibition traveled to Paris, where it was shown at the Musée de la Mode, also with long lines.

- In the spring of 2003, the first Louis Vuitton collection inspired by the Jackie Kennedy style went on sale to the public.

- In the spring of 2003, Louis Vuitton presented its autumn and winter collection for 2003/2004 to the press and store buyers. Once more the understated early-1960s style was one of the themes of the collection.

- In the spring of 2003, *Textile View* suggested themes for its designer readers with regard to the spring/summer 2004 season. This time the focus was on summer clothing in the Kennedy style.

- In the autumn of 2003, several trendy fashion magazines had headlines like "Watch Out for 1960s Style" with references to the Louis Vuitton collection. The collection that had been presented in spring 2003 was then for sale in the Louis Vuitton stores.

- In some of the spring/summer collections for 2004 presented at fashion fairs in the autumn of 2003, other designers had also been inspired by the Jackie Kennedy style.

That was it. The following season there was no hint of Jackie Kennedy at the fashion houses or the companies that copy them. Suddenly the Jackie Kennedy style was over.

The comeback of the Jackie Kennedy style was a typical seasonal fashion fad that had a short time span and no long-lasting influence on fashion history (though not typical of fads, this particular fad can be said—together with many other different seasonal fashion fads—to be a variation on the overall nostalgia theme that was prevalent at the time). Each season there may be 5 or 10, or even more, seasonal fashion fads like the comeback of the Jackie Kennedy style that typically get a lot of sudden coverage in the fashion magazines. However, these seasonal fashion fads created by a designer or a brand quickly become outdated when they have been copied by other fashion designers and when they have been written about in the fashion magazines for one or two seasons. Neither the fashion industry nor the fashion press has any interest in keeping this kind of fashion fad alive because both believe that such a fad cannot be used to sell more clothing or more magazines after one or two seasons.

A fad can also be called a craze, rage, or mania, words that when used in other situations often indicate something short term. There are different kinds of fads in different industries. In the fashion industry, new designs are presented twice a year, which gives a certain rhythm to the fads, whereas in, say, the car industry, new cars are introduced only at the yearly car fairs, which creates another rhythm (as does the price level of the products).

Ultimately, all fads have the same characteristics: they are very short stories that revolve around some new, innovative products. In this case, the products appeal to the trendsetters, but they never get far beyond a very tiny crowd. They often have appeal only for less than a year. They are sometimes heavily marketed by the industry or, in the case of fashion, by the fashion magazines. This is all very predictable, and each fad is quickly forgotten because something new comes along all the time.

A really large crowd became aware of Scandinavian furniture design in the 1950s. From 1954 to 1957, an exhibition called "Design in Scandinavia" traveled to 22 cities in the United States and Canada. Some 650,000 people visited this furniture show, and many more people read about it in newspapers and magazines. Scandinavian furniture style became more than a fad;

it became a trend. Then and now exhibitions and media certainly play a huge role in how changes in style and taste evolve, though many stores now have the same qualities as exhibitions, because going into a store today can sometimes be like visiting a design show. To get more clues to how the changes in style and taste happen we can investigate another story that took place later in the twentieth century.

In 1989 a then little-known leather accessories company called Prada in Milan, Italy, introduced a new clothing collection with simple, understated designs to the public. The Prada collections for the following seasons showcased a sleek, understated style that was suddenly talked about a lot in the fashion world. *Time* magazine wrote about "Understated Art," describing the clothes as "unassertive, combining traditional good manners and an ultramodern industrial sleekness." In 1979 Prada had introduced backpacks made of a tough, military-spec black nylon, and a black nylon version of a tote bag had been introduced in 1985, also in the same understated style.

Other designers, like Italian Giorgio Armani and his American colleague Calvin Klein, had been creating clothing in an under-stated style in the 1980s, but it was with the launch of the Prada clothing collections of the early 1990s that minimalism suddenly became all the rage in fashion. The minimalists used many high-tech fabrics, and the colors were neutral, with beige, gray, and black predominating. And these colors were still predominating in the late 1990s. The understated style had become widely pop-ular, not only in fashion, but also in home furnishings and inte-rior design for both private homes and stores. In architecture, there was a renewed interest in mid-twentieth-century modernist—and minimalist—houses built by architects like Philip Johnson and Richard Neutra.

In the mid-1990s, the Calvin Klein flagship store on Madison Avenue in New York City became the quintessence of 1990s minimalist style. The space was designed by British architect John Pawson, who used furniture by Donald Judd in the store. The minimalist style of Giorgio Armani's and Calvin Klein's stores then inspired many other store owners and designers to decorate in the same understated style. This understated style also dominated the interiors of the San Francisco–headquartered mainstream clothing store chains Gap and Banana Republic. In her memoir of being a *New York Post* relationship columnist, Bridget Harrison in 2000 described how a Chelsea apartment was "painted in a trendy hotel off-white."

So the story of 1990s minimalism and the revival of the Jackie Kennedy style are different from each other, but incidentally they have the same historical roots. It is not as if either style was brand new to the world when it was introduced in the early 1990s and early twenty-first century, respectively. The historical roots of minimalism in interior design go back a long time. In the United States, Shaker communities from Maine to Kentucky had preferred a simple style for more than 200 years. The sleek modernist movement in architecture that started in the 1930s was also about simplicity and had also involved furniture design. In the early 1960s, American furniture designer and artist Donald Judd became the founding father of minimalist art, which influenced many creative people. Also in the early 1960s then curator Sam Wagstaff staged a photo exhibition called *Black, White + Gray* at the Wadsworth Atheneum, Hartford, the largest art museum in Connecticut. The exhibition showed black-and-white photographs and "sent shock waves through popular culture and heralded fashion's embrace of Minimalist aesthetics." *Vogue* magazine published an eight-page fashion article with *Black, White + Gray* as the backdrop. As Wagstaff proved again and again in his life, "he was always ahead of the curve," according to James Crump, who has made a documentary about the Yale-educated Wagstaff.

Later in the 1960s, clothing style was changing from simplicity to "Flower Power." But in interior design one small group of gay men now started embracing a very uncolorful style. In the late 1960s, an architect named Paul Rudolph, who was then dean of the department of architecture at Yale University, had designed an apartment for himself in New Haven, Connecticut. This apartment became a design classic; "its clean, uncluttered spaces set the tone for the whole Minimalist movement in interior design," according to a biography of the late American fashion designer Perry Ellis, who also lived in the apartment for a while. Paul Rudolph created a unique style in interior design—the sleek minimalist style. Like Sam Wagstaff and Perry Ellis, he also happened to be gay (which is a characteristic of a considerable number of the men mentioned in this book).

In 1971, Calvin Klein (with the help of then up-and-coming interior designer John Stedila) moved into an apartment that was "the cutting edge of the seventies minimalist movement," according to a biography of Klein. The apartment was later featured in the *New York Times.* In 1974, another fashion designer, the late Roy Halston, bought an apartment with both the interior and the furniture designed by Paul Rudolph. The walls were white, and there was no clutter and no little knickknacks anywhere. The furniture was geometric, and the dominating furniture colors were gray and putty.

Both Perry Ellis and Calvin Klein later decided to have the showrooms of their companies designed in a simple, minimal style as well. Calvin Klein opened his minimalist showroom in 1977. In 1979 Perry Ellis opened his showroom, where the colors were mostly beige, typical of the minimalist style. The Ellis showroom ended up being featured in major publications like *Architectural Digest* and newspapers like the *New York Times.*

In the late 1970s in the Los Angeles area three restaurants gave birth to a new style in restaurant interiors. One of the restaurants was West Beach Café in Venice Beach. The interiors of the restaurants were white, off-white, and beige, a completely different style from the stuffed interior design style of restaurants at the time. The waiters at Michael's wore cream-colored suits, radically different from the black suits normally worn by waiters. The style became known as "the California look."

In 1981, across the Atlantic, with Austrian-Italian designer Ettore Sotsass at the helm, a group of international and Italian designers and architects had founded the Memphis design group in Milan, then Italy's emerging fashion capital. These designers created a furniture design style that was colorful, decorative, eclectic, and playful—the exact opposite of minimalism. The Memphis style also caught on internationally. At the same time, *Dallas* and *Dynasty* were the most popular TV shows on both sides of the Atlantic, with characters who wore very glamorous clothing, as a big part of the population did.

Then in 1984 a group of Milan-based designers decided to create design that was completely different from that typical of the early 1980s. The designers in the Zeus partnership—just like some New York interior designers—wanted design to be understated and minimalist, whether they were designing clothing, furniture, or interior spaces. The Zeus group launched a furniture collection dominated by thin black metal. Giorgio Armani, then Italy's best-known designer, also based in Milan, asked the Zeus designers to design his new showroom and his stores in Italy in Zeus's signature minimalist style. This happened between 1984 and 1988. And in the late 1980s the first Prada clothing collection was launched with lots of black nylon. In the early 1990s, designer Bill Stumpf was designing a new office chair for furniture manufacturer Herman Miller that was the signature black color but otherwise was completely different from the existing office chairs. This chair was sleek, and instead of leather or fabric, a thin elastic mesh was stretched tight over the plastic frame. It was typical minimalist style.

The big difference between the return of the Jackie Kennedy style and the "arrival" of the minimalist style is the process that took place before the style came to the attention of the world. The minimalist style that exploded in the 1990s had been simmering among a creative group of people for some time. With the Jackie Kennedy style, a few editors had an idea for a theme in the fashion collections. With the minimalist style, there had been a social process going on among a wider group of creative people. Different kinds of creative people had been able to register that something new was happening by observing one another. They may also have had conversations with one another, although since they were competitors, many of them would probably not have had personal contact. It was more a case of creative people "instinctively" liking the same style and sharing the same taste. They are also people who observe a lot because they are visually oriented. This is a clear hint that the trend process is often about observing (combined with reading about the new style in newspapers and magazines). This process of simmering and observing is one of the first clues to why minimalism more or less became the epitome of 1990s style.

Something that is going to affect a lot of people has to be seen as part of a process. It will not just pop up out of the blue. It takes time for the style and taste of a big part of a country's population to change. It simply cannot happen in a short time. So the first lead in this detective story is to be aware of the simmering process leading up to a change in style or taste.

The second clue is that if the same style becomes evident in different product categories, such as clothing and home furnishings, it is in all probability an emerging trend and not just a fad.

A third clue comes from watching what is going on in mainstream style. When what was the newest style becomes mainstream, the trendsetters will react to its popularity by moving to something completely different. When you are a trendsetter this "comes naturally," so to speak. When fashion and interiors photographer Micky Hoyle from South Africa was interviewed about his white-and-cream colored apartment in Cape Town he said: "My former home was very bright and had many colors. This apartment is the absolute opposite, even though it was not a conscious choice. It was just what felt right."

That style and taste change from one end of the spectrum to the other is not news—in fact, it's rather an old story. In his book *History of Art*, H. W. Janson writes, "[In the 1770s] the anti-Rococo trend in painting was first a matter of content rather than style." After the asymmetrical and curvy rococo style, with its many naturalistic influences, came the neoclassical style, which was its complete opposite: symmetrical and linear, based on ancient Greek and Roman style.

For much of the twentieth century, changes in style of dress, furniture, cars, and other designed objects followed this pattern. For instance, the changes in women's dress style can be seen by flipping through books on women's fashion design covering the twentieth century. In some decades the clothing style was simple, while in others it was more ornamental and decorative.

The art nouveau style of the first decade of the twentieth century was very voluptuous, featuring decorated dresses with many details. In the 1920s, the Charleston-style dresses became much simpler, with fewer colors. This simple style continued into the 1930s, when the focus was on practicality and functionality. During World War II in the 1940s there were limitations on textile production, and decorative details were reduced even further.

After the war, fashion designers could again use more textiles, and the French designer Christian Dior created not only an instant hit but also a trend when he introduced his New Look style in 1947, featuring big skirts. With the war over, many women were really hungry for the opposite of what they had been wearing during the war. So a more voluptuous show of fabric was popular.

After a decade, clothing style became simpler again, and it was this style, which was favored by First Lady Jacqueline Kennedy, that dominated the first half of the 1960s. In the United States, Oleg Cassini was one of the leading designers working in the understated style that Jacqueline Kennedy liked. In France, designers like André Courrêges, Paco Rabanne, and Pierre Cardin designed futuristic yet simple clothing inspired by space exploration.

With youth culture dominating the social scene in the second half of the 1960s, many young people dressed to snub the establishment. The hippie style that emerged in San Francisco became a trend in most Western countries. In the late 1960s and the 1970s, clothing gradually became more and more casual. In the early 1970s, the dominant style was the Flower Power style, with many colors and decorative patterns. In the 1980s, clothes became romantic and glamorous, with lots of shoulder padding. Many TV viewers were following the glamorous design visible in TV shows such as *Dallas* and *Dynasty* or liking the nostalgic design of American designer Ralph Lauren.

Then in the early 1990s the Italian fashion house Prada introduced a new minimalist style, with only a few neutral colors and high-tech fabrics. By the late 1990s, beige and other neutral colors and minimalist style had become mainstream.

In the spring of 1997, in trendsetting fashion stores such as New York Style Exchange in Los Angeles and Voyage in London, designers introduced floral patterns and bohemian styles. At the end of the 1990s, the style was retro, inspired by the 1960s and 1970s and spearheaded by Tom Ford, then artistic director of Gucci, which had a major comeback in the mid-1990s. In 1996 and again in 1997, Gucci introduced a more colorful look in its collections, underlining the trend toward more colorful and decorated clothing styles that ended the century.

The more colorful style that Gucci introduced coincided with the launch of *Nest*, a magazine that championed ornamentation in interior design. This was certainly not mainstream in 1997. Since the beginning of the 1990s, the minimalist trend in interior design had spread and had become popular in store design in many retail chains, and the style was featured in interior design magazines all over the Western world. The trendsetters, however, at that time preferred the style that *Nest* represented.

By just looking at fashion style (with a bit of interior design) throughout the twentieth century, we can see a pattern of changes from one style to its complete opposite. There is a sort of pendulum—a change from the style at one end of the design spectrum to a style that is at the opposite end of the design spectrum, as seen in Figure 1.1.

So, to get back to the third clue in trend spotting, it often seems to be that the exact opposite of an existing popular or mainstream style is the starting point for a new trend. There are many more clues to what happens inside the trend process, and they will be discussed in the following chapters.

MEGATRENDS

Before going into more detail on how a trend grows, it is worth noticing that not only are people using the word *trend* more and more, but people in different professions are also using it in many different contexts. But regardless of what it means to different professions, the concept of change is always part of the definition.

There are many other types of changes besides trends; shifts in politics, the economy, technology, and culture, for example, do not necessarily follow the same process of change that we see in matters of design and style, although people will also use the term *trend* to refer to them. But if we look at changes in technology, politics, the economy, and culture, it can be argued that changes in these areas take place over longer time periods and are more complex—indeed, if they were fast, we would call them revolutions.

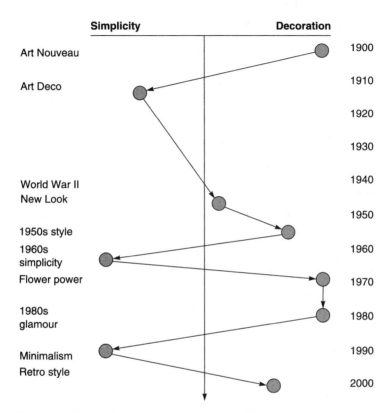

Figure 1.1 Oscillating trends in women's clothing styles in the twentieth century

Because of an awareness that there are these different kinds of changes, some people use the word *megatrend* when discussing cultural, economic, political, or technological shifts that are just about to happen, with the implication that these megatrends will affect all or almost all of society. American futurist John Naisbitt was one of the first to use the word in his 1982 book *Megatrends*. His 1990 book *Megatrends 2000* highlighted 10 megatrends. Three of them were "The 1990s: The Decade of Women in Leadership,"

"Religious Revival of the Third Millennium," and "Renaissance in the Arts."

In connection with the last of these megatrends, he wrote that new art museums were opening on almost all continents, and there were more museumgoers, more operagoers, more theatergoers, and so on, than ever before. The number of performing arts organizations nearly doubled during the last three decades of the twentieth century. In fact, around the year 2000, important new art museums were still opening, among them the Guggenheim Bilbao in Spain, the Guggenheim Hermitage Museum in Las Vegas, the Tate Modern in London, and the J. Paul Getty Center in Los Angeles. The number of people visiting museums had been setting new records in the 1980s, according to Naisbitt. In the beginning of the twenty-first century, long lines of people waiting to get in to see museum shows were common. Some museums started selling advance tickets for specific dates and time slots to limit the lines—like when you go to the theater or the opera.

This kind of change is completely different from a trend. Megatrends last longer, they affect many different aspects of society, and they involve a complex process that often includes politics, the economy, and technology. Megatrends often have some lasting influence on societies and are not very predictable. Also, to describe the anatomy of megatrends would involve just about every social science there is, and probably take a whole series of books.

THE NEED FOR STYLE

Is the fact that modern consumers are interested in trends in and of itself a trend? No, it is actually a major social change, and one that was predicted by the late U.S. psychologist Abraham Maslow, who is best known for his theory of the Hierarchy of Needs.

Maslow's core idea is that people have essential needs—the bottom of the hierarchy—that must be fulfilled before they can begin to think of fulfilling the needs at the top of the hierarchy. In other words, we humans must have food and shelter and strong bonds with others before we can start thinking about what style of sweater we want to wear or how we want to decorate our homes.

From reading Maslow's original texts, it appears that he recognized that humans' needs are more nuanced than simply having sustenance and shelter and social needs fulfilled before they can have self-actualization. In fact, his original text indicated the following seven needs:

7. Self-actualization need
6. Aesthetic needs
5. Cognitive needs
4. Esteem needs
3. Belongingness and love needs
2. Safety needs
1. Physiological needs

Maslow admitted that science knew least about the aesthetic needs. But a brief look way back in human history shows that we have always been preoccupied with matters of style and taste. Think of the cave paintings discovered in the south of France. Clearly, the earliest humans did not spend all their time hunting for food or resting.

With this thinking, it makes sense that consumers at different steps in the hierarchy will have different interests in style and design. Consumers are more preoccupied with style and taste when they are well-off because then they are at the top of Hierarchy of Needs. And this preoccupation with style and taste is not likely to change unless the economy or the political system changes radically. However, if the economy continues to evolve the way it has evolved during the twentieth century (with more people being well-off), the interest in style and taste will only grow stronger.

SPOTTING A TREND

So with the growing interest in style and taste, it makes sense for us to want to know how to spot new trends. One key element in recognizing a trend is to look for signs that some aspect of human behavior is changing. The signs may not be very obvious, but they are there. They were there in the 1990s when drink tastes changed.

In the 1990s, the big breweries made the mistake of over-looking the signs that beer drinking was apparently becoming untrendy. Statistics show that in the 1990s, there was a decreasing demand for beer in many Western countries. For several years Gallup has asked the U.S. population about its drinking preferences. In 1992, 47 percent gave beer as their favorite adult beverage. In 2005, only 36 percent named beer as their favorite adult beverage. In Germany, beer consumption fell by 20 percent in the two decades from 1980 to 2000, and in the beginning of the twenty-first century it fell even more. In Great Britain, the number of people drinking beer decreased by 5 percent during the 1990s.

In 2005, Gallup News Service reported that one of the biggest trends that Gallup saw in drinking patterns between 1992 and 2005 was a "crumbling of the once-dominant positioning of beer among adults. It appears that young adults are trading in their beer mugs for martini glasses, in droves." Beer consumption in the 18–29 age group had been going down, and the percentage saying that they preferred liquor more than doubled, from 13 percent to 32 percent.

Early in the 1990s and certainly by the mid-1990s, there were many signs that beer consumption would decrease—most of them related to changes in people's behavior:

- Trendsetters began to drink cocktails in the beginning of the 1990s. In Los Angeles, a new type of cocktail lounge, such as Liquid Kitty, Goldfingers, and Lava Lounge, became the prototype of a new kind of nightspot all over the Western world. And in 1997, *Elle* wrote: "Cocktails and martinis are in."
- Illegal drugs such as ecstasy became popular in many nightspots. Users did not need to get drunk and therefore preferred bottled water to beer and hard liquor.
- Wine became still more popular.
- An increasing consumer focus on healthy living and low-fat products made some people stop drinking beer.
- Cafés became more popular, taking over from bars as social meeting places.
- Young consumers were becoming more individualistic and were not interested in buying uniform mass products (as represented by the big domestic breweries).
- Many new liquor brands with interesting new bottle designs were introduced.
- There was a huge focus on product development in the hard liquor industry. Many flavors were added to traditional spirits: first lemon and orange, and later cranberry and other flavors.
- Many ready-to-drink beverages (a mix of soft drinks and liquor products) were introduced.

All these signs were out in the open. It would have been possible to put them together and make a qualified prediction that there would be a decreasing demand for beer. Of course, spotting the trend does not mean that you have to react to the information, or at least not right away. For instance, if you are representing a big company with a satisfactory market, you may want to be very sure of the trend before you start changing strategies; however, if you are a small business or an entrepreneur, you may want to react right away and take on the new market that is emerging.

The big breweries experienced another change in their market at the beginning of the twenty-first century: the market's response to consumers' decreasing interest in beer from the large breweries was the opening of microbreweries, which was a distinct new development in the beer market in the beginning of the twenty-first century that satisfied the need for non-mass-produced beer. The trend had already begun in the 1980s with the founding of The Boston Beer Company whose first beer was Samuel Adams Boston Lager.

As beer became less and less popular, wine was becoming more and more popular. As the taste in adult beverages changed in the wine industry's favor, this meant that wine became mainstream, and the trendsetters then reacted to this. In the 1990s, there was a change in favor of wine from certain districts, countries, and types of grapes. To quote *Time* magazine: "Like hemlines and flares, wine varieties come in and out of style. One year, Chardonnay or Pinot Gris find acceptance; the next they're passé." So according to *Time*, there are also fads in the wine industry. In the beginning of the twenty-first century there was, for instance, an interest in older varieties, like Malbec and the hybrid Incrocio Manzoni. Depending on the process surrounding a new variety, it will become either a fad or a trend, just as in fashion and in interior design.

The one sure thing is that style and taste change from time to time. Sometimes the explanation for a new change will be obvious, sometimes it will be complex, and often there are many reasons why a change takes place. But in all cases the change occurs because of human behavior. There are only a few nonhuman influences that make changes happen—natural catastrophes, for example. Almost all changes in style and taste are caused by human beings. So to the extent that we can understand and explain human behavior, we can also understand and explain trends.

Many people believe that trends are mysterious or inexplicable phenomena that nobody really understands. But actually trends are more predictable than most people think. Their predictability arises from the fact that they are sociological processes that involve human beings, and human behavior in the aggregate can—sometimes—be quite predictable.

TREND-SPOTTING CLUES

When we want to spot new and emerging trends, we can start by looking at the trend characteristics that have been covered in this chapter:

- Trends are always created by people, so trend spotting is about watching people who create or are preoccupied with new and innovative styles.
- Trend spotting is possible because the key element in the development of any trend is observing, either in real life or in the media. What the trendsetters observe, we can also observe.
- A new trend has almost always been simmering for some time before it starts boiling.
- If a new, innovative style is visible in two (or more) industries at the same time, it is likely to be a trend.
- A new trend is often a reaction to what has become mainstream or what has been on the market for many years.
- Changes in style often go from one end of the style spectrum to the other.
- To be a successful trend spotter, you have to watch out for discrete signs of change and then put them into the analytical framework that is presented in this book.

2

THE CAST OF CHARACTERS

TREND CREATORS AND TRENDSETTERS

9 723456 485247

Changes in style and taste may often appear to come "out of the blue" and leave some people wondering who actually decided that something is popular to wear, listen to, or eat. The fact of the matter is that it is always some very real human beings who make it happen, and they are the main characters in the story we are chronicling.

The prime movers in any trend process will often go by different names, for instance, inventors, innovators, pioneers, or entrepreneurs. They create new products or invent new styles or begin doing something in a completely new way. Their role in this detective story is very well known. Their stories have been told often, and in many cases they are the heroes of some great stories of innovation and entrepreneurship. However, not all inventors, entrepreneurs, and professional innovators (for instance, designers) create trends. In many cases what is created will not cause a major change in style and taste that affects large numbers of people. But if a new product or style is adopted by the trendsetters, the style will become a trend, and an innovator or inventor will become a trend creator.

So while the trend creators are often well-known heroes, the trendsetters are typically not. Their names are not known, and their stories have not really been told. In fact, their part in this story is the great mystery. Few people know what goes on in the process that turns an inventor, innovator, or entrepreneur into a trend creator. But in this part of the process, the trendsetters are the protagonists.

If we want to know who the trendsetters are, it seems logical to start by studying some real-life trends. Then we can learn whether the trendsetters stand out in any distinct ways.

One such real-life trend has its origin in India. For centuries women in India and Indian immigrants in other countries have used henna to decorate their hands. This decorative technique is called *mehndi*. In the late 1990s, mehndi suddenly became a trend in Western countries among people outside of the immigrant groups who had been doing mehndi for decades and decades. Suddenly Indian women could be credited as being the original creators of a trend. But this is only because there are trendsetters such as Claire Ramsey from New York City.

In 1996, Ramsey started painting mehndi on her hands. Ramsey later recounted to the Danish newspaper *BT* how she first became interested in mehndi: "I was traveling in India and saw Indian women decorated with mehndi everywhere. When I came back to New York City, I found henna color in a small Indian store. I only painted a small pattern on the top of my hand. I felt it would look ridiculous if I decorated the entire hand, just like Indian women do. And I also wanted to create my own style."

One day that year, when Ramsey was sitting in a New York City café, people started asking her about the henna tattoos, and some of the New Yorkers who observed them started having henna tattoos painted on their hands. In 1997, a book on street culture mentioned that mehndi was a new trend. The same year, you could get mehndi painted on your hands at the trendy cafés of the Spanish island of Ibiza, which was popular with many trendsetters at the time. When celebrities like Prince and Madonna were seen in magazines with mehndi, they were among the trendsetters. In 1999, *National Geographic* magazine wrote that mehndi was "a very cool thing to do." The magazine quoted Los Angeles–based artist and mehndi artisan Pascal Giacomini as saying, "Now it's hugely popular—in Japan, Argentina, Sweden, Greece. My Guatemalan maid does it."

At that time, Pascal Giacomini had developed a mehndi kit and was selling it in more than a hundred different outlets. The giant cosmetics companies also hopped onto the mehndi bandwagon. Among others, Estée Lauder introduced mehndi kits.

Claire Ramsey is the prototype of a modern trendsetter. As she told the newspaper, "I often get ideas from what I like myself. I think first and foremost of whether I like it myself or not." What Claire Ramsey says is typical of trendsetters: they do not care what other people think when they adopt something new.

When the style or products of trend creators become commercialized, it is the trendsetters who start using or buying these products or services before everybody else. And it is only when someone actually starts to use the innovative product, design, or style that there is a chance for it to spread. In other words, someone always has to be the first, and trendsetters are by definition the first to adopt a *new* innovative product, design, or style. The one crucial factor in the spreading of a new style or taste is its acceptance by the trendsetters.

Another such trendsetter is Julia Sador, a London-based DJ working under the DJ name Princess Julia. A friend of hers, the musician and writer Aiden Shaw, wrote in his memoir: "When Julia constructed a look, she nailed it with precision and detail. She was always at least six months (sometimes a year or more) ahead of what you saw on catwalks or in fashion magazines." Judged by the many photos of her on her DJ Web site, she appears to be a true chameleon who changes style often. She has been wearing new clothing styles the exact moment they have become available.

Sometimes it is obvious who is the trend creator and who is the trendsetter; sometimes it is not. But the principal distinction is that trend creators have created something new, while trendsetters have been the first to adopt the new.

But how do we identify the trendsetters as a group? The examples of Claire Ramsey and Julia Sador could indicate that young people play a role (in this book young is defined as being under 30). In music, for example, there is no doubt that young people also have been major trend creators and trendsetters in the twentieth century. Let's start our detective work by looking into some of the prominent youth cultures that pioneered a new style and new tastes in music. What is typical of youth cultures is that they are mostly fairly anonymous as individuals when they are pioneering a new style.

THE YOUNG

Poet and punk rock singer Patti Smith was one of the pioneers in punk rock, and she also played a role in the creation of the punk look. In fact, she is credited with initiating the trend for ripped or shredded clothing. It was in the late 1960s that she tore apart both T-shirts and blue jeans. During the punk movement in the 1970s, many others started doing the same, some piecing their clothing together with safety pins. They became known as punks.

Patti Smith was among the first to play punk rock, doing so even before the term was used to define the then-emerging sound, but she was not the trend creator. In music, she was a trendsetter. "It was a real reaction against disco music and the glitter-rock thing. Our lyrics were much more sophisticated, and we weren't into artifice at all," she said later of this period in the mid-1970s. This statement confirms what was also pointed out in Chapter 1: new trends are often reactions to an existing style or taste.

If we go back a little further than the 1960s, one of the first characteristics of the emerging teenage culture after World War II was a different way of dressing. Before the war, there were clothes for children and clothes for adults. But after the war, the apparel industry began manufacturing clothes just for teenagers, and designers and (in many cases) nondesigners like Patti Smith created new styles.

Before World War II, most young people entered the labor force when they were in their teens. They typically started working with a lot of grown-ups and mostly emulated them. But as more technology came into use, there was a need for a better-educated workforce. From the 1950s on, therefore, more and more people went to college. For the first time in history (outside of the army), many young people became part of communities that included only other people in their own age bracket. In his autobiography *Hell's Angel*, biker Ralph "Sonny" Barger writes: "I organized a small street corner club in 1954 when I was still at [high school and was 13 years old]. We wore our jackets with the collars up and had 'Earth Angels' embroidered on the back. The Earth Angels never did anything special. We didn't stand for anything. It was just something to belong to. . . . It was all about belonging to a group of people just like you."

At that time, the biker culture, with black leather jackets, blue jeans, and engineer's boots, had already been created. Young Ralph Barger was a trendsetter in the process of spreading the biker look. That was the same year that Marlon Brando sported the biker look in the hit movie *On the Waterfront*, and one year before James Dean wore a leather jacket in *Rebel without a Cause*.

In his book *Vietnam: The War at Home*, the historian Thomas Powers writes that in the beginning of the 1960s, students at the big U.S. universities began to dress in the beat style, with blue jeans, long hair, and beards. However, the male hippies were not the first to let their hair grow. The long-haired style for men can be traced back to the 1950s bikers. Barger describes this in his autobiography when he writes about his friend Terry the Tramp: "Looking back, he was a trendsetter. Between the beatniks and the hippies, Tramp grew his hair real long [and] wore a full beard." From San Francisco, the long-haired hippie style spread to the rest of the Western world—and became a highly vocal and visible movement in many countries in the 1960s and 1970s. Many of the original Hells Angels bikers from the San Francisco Bay area sported tattoos—and this became a trend decades later (which we'll explore later in this chapter).

From the 1950s on, it was often young people who needed to differentiate themselves from grown-ups and by doing so created new styles. Often young people's way of dressing inspired the fashion designers in their work. This was certainly the case in the 1990s, when hip-hop became a global style influencing music, language, and clothing.

The roots of hip-hop go back to the 1970s, to the poor African American boys and men in large U.S. cities. At that time, many of those cities had developed ghettos that were characterized by decay. This was particularly the case in the African American neighborhoods of New York City. Violence and crime were rampant, and many gang members inevitably were jailed. The men who were doing time influenced other young people in their community in terms of their way of dressing. For instance, in jail you are not allowed to wear a belt—for safety reasons. This inspired friends and family of the jailed men to also wear trousers without a belt, with the trousers often hanging low on the hips.

Musically, it was a DJ from Jamaica with the artist name DJ Kool Herc who played an important role in the emerging hip-hop culture. In the mid-1970s he started organizing street parties in the South Bronx. The Jamaican DJ noticed that the dancing teenagers especially liked certain musical passages. Therefore, he introduced the "merry-go-round": he put two copies of the same record on two parallel turntables playing at the same time, and thus he could prolong the most popular music rhythm breaks.

Another Bronx DJ called Grandmaster Flash is credited with inventing scratching, another hip-hop musical invention. Scratching is the technique of audibly rotating a disk back and forth while the turntable is running. It led to the creation of a whole new staccato sound, which in turn inspired a whole new way of dancing, with acrobatic and staccato movements—a dancing style that we know today as break dancing. Break dancing was done in the streets, and soon a ritualized form of break dancing competitions emerged. (One of the most spectacular steps in break dancing is head spinning—standing on your head and spinning.) The break dancers' clothing was inspired by their physical activities: they wore functional activewear and sneakers.

When DJ Kool Herc was busy being a DJ, he needed another person—a sort of toastmaster—who could urge on the dancers and party guests. The Jamaican toasters, who had incited the audience when reggae music was first invented in Jamaica, inspired him. With the introduction of toasters, yet another musical style emerged: rap music. Rapping (speaking in verse with music) also turned into a competition and a way to show off how good you were at improvising with words.

Until 1979, rapping was exclusively a live musical genre. It was not until Sylvia Robinson, an independent record company owner, put three rappers together in a studio and named them the Sugarhill Gang that the first rap record was made. The group's single "Rapper's Delight" was a big hit, selling more than two million copies worldwide in the next few years.

Another early successful rapping group was Run-DMC. In 1983 it released the single "It's Like That." In 1986 Run DMC got a megahit with the single "My Adidas," which more or less canonized Adidas sneakers among hip-hoppers—and later among many other young people. By the beginning of the twentieth-first century rap was an established music genre, performed in French, Japanese, Danish, and many other languages.

The term *hip-hop* was coined by Afrika Bambaataa, the founder of the Universal Zulu Nation, now the world's oldest and largest grassroots hip-hop organization. The word was coined to describe a whole lifestyle, including music, clothing, and language, as well as events and gatherings. Together with activewear training suits, luxury-brand clothing became an important ingredient in the hip-hop style. At the same time, the hip-hoppers did not deny their roots. Many African Americans have traditionally worn gold jewelry and bright colors. This style is about looking sharper and richer than you actually are. So hip-hop style became a mix of activewear, luxury brands, and oversized gold jewelry.

As hip-hoppers aspired to look like rich people, they took a keen interest in the preppy clothes that were very fashionable in the 1980s. This had a huge influence on a relatively new brand called Tommy Hilfiger, a brand with a style similar to that of Ralph Lauren, but less expensive. As the African American hip-hoppers became more and more visible, becoming the idols of Caucasian middle-class teenagers, Tommy Hilfiger became one of the popular brands of the 1990s, first among hip-hoppers and later among young people outside of the African American neighborhoods, increasing the brand's sales volume inside and outside of the United States.

In Japan, Tokyo has one of the world's most visually expressive youth cultures. This is why many fashion designers in the 1980s started traveling to Tokyo for inspiration. For many years Tokyo's youth culture scene has revolved around the Harajuku train station, which has given its name to the phenomenon "Harajuku girls." These teenage girls (and sometimes boys) make a point of dressing in colorful and kitschy clothing styles. The Harajuku girl style has inspired singer Gwen Stefani in her video imagery and styling and her "Harajuku Lovers Tour" in 2005.

It is not often that we can identify who first thought of a new style. And unless it is a matter of copyright, it does not matter who gets the credit officially. But if a style is inspired by the street or very visible at a music festival, there is a chance that it will be noticed by multiple trendsetters—giving it a better chance of becoming a trend. A product, design, or style that can be observed by numerous people at the same time is more likely to spread and become a trend.

Youth culture and *street culture* are very loose terms that can be used to refer to many different kinds of groups and subcultures. But young people certainly seem to play a key role in the creation and advancement of many trends. However, they are not the only ones who play that role. On that note we also have clues about designers and other creative people from Chapter 1 to work with.

DESIGNERS

The concept of fashion—of clothes that are made in a certain popular style—began in France in the mid-1800s. The originator was an Englishman, Charles Frederick Worth, who had settled in Paris in 1845.

Worth was born into a poor middle-class family in the English town of Bourne in 1825. When he was only 11, he began an apprenticeship as a painter, but two years later he got a job in a fabric store in London. When he was 20, Worth went to Paris with very little money, and speaking even less French. After a while, he learned the language and landed a job with Gagelin and Opigez, then the most fashionable fabric store in Paris. He was employed at that store for 12 years, first as a sales clerk and later as a dressmaker.

The way Worth made dresses was completely different from the way traditional tailors did so. Instead of asking the client what she wanted, he began by looking at the possibilities of the fabric and the person who was going to wear the dress.

Together with his wife, Worth opened his own tailor's shop in 1858. There many wealthy customers, and for them, the economy was good. As a result, Worth soon had a profitable business. When a customer, the wife of the Austrian ambassador, wore a Worth dress at the court of Napoleon III, Empress Eugénie asked her who had made the dress. With a warm recommendation from the ambassador's wife, Worth soon became dressmaker to the imperial court.

Worth always stuck to the principle that *he* decided what the dress he was creating was to look like. Even with his most aristocratic customers, Worth did not hesitate to dictate how the dresses he made should look.

Worth created the modern fashion designer. He died in 1885, and in the twentieth century, it was no longer the customers who decided what clothing should look like. That decision was—and is—made by fashion designers. The difference between being a traditional tailor and being a fashion designer is that a tailor asks the customers what they want, whereas a designer has his or her own idea of what to create.

This does not mean that fashion designers do not interact with and adapt to the tastes of their customers. To some extent they do, but they do not engage in traditional market research. Instead, the fashion industry is very conscious of trends and the existence of trendsetters, and designers use this knowledge to stay in touch with the market or even to try to stay ahead of it.

Each decade since the beginning of the twentieth century has seen exceptionally creative designers who have had enormous influence on clothing. In the late 1940s, it was the French designer Christian Dior, whose influence was visible on both sides of the Atlantic. In 1947 he launched his famous "New Look" collection in Paris, and the following year he opened a store in New York. The writer Edmund White has written in his autobiography that his mother, who was living in a small town in Texas, was wearing New Look style dresses a couple of years later.

When Yves Saint Laurent a decade later was the designer for Dior, the inspiration went from the United States to Europe.

In 1960 he created a collection that was inspired by the beats (more on the beats in Chapter 4).

In the beginning of the twenty-first century designers can find inspiration among a wide variety of sources and groups, often making the designers trendsetters rather than trend creators. In England, one variation of the hip-hop style is called "ghetto fabulous" and is popular among African immigrants in London. Phoebe Philo, then a design assistant at the French fashion house Chloé, was one of the first trendsetters to adopt the ghetto fabulous look. To *Vogue* she said: "I like the look because it's . . . really sexy. I'll go down to Brixton, Willesden or Harlesden to buy the clothes—fantastic string vests and dresses—where there are also great hairdressers who do extensions and hair weaves, with nail boutiques in the back." In 2001 this glamorous look was interpreted in the Chloé collection, with big gold earrings and wide gold belts.

The influence of fashion designers is not limited to clothing. When he was a creative director for Dior Homme, designer Hedi Slimane was a trend creator in men's hairstyles in the beginning of the twenty-first century. It was Slimane who first had his hair cut in a Mohawk hairstyle (the hair is swept up toward the top from the sides). Hairdressers in London began copying this style, and in 2002 celebrities like British soccer star David Beckham and later British pop singer Robbie Williams were seen with the Mohawk hairstyle. (David Beckham and Hedi Slimane are both friends with Janet Street Porter, a writer and broadcaster.) In 2005 the *New York Times* journalist Charlie LeDuff had a Mohawk haircut while attending the Burning Man festival in Nevada. But as he found out, so did almost everybody else. Slimane has told *The New Yorker* that he abandoned his faux-hawk hairstyle when he encountered one on a desk clerk at a hotel in Prague. After Charlie LeDuff had spotted Mohawks en masse at the Burning Man festival he pointed out that "no matter how you slice it, if everyone's doing it, it ain't cool."

ARTISTS

We can also look for clues among other creative people, a category that first and foremost includes artists. Artists have a long history of being trend creators and trendsetters. There are really two types of artists: creative artists and performing artists. The first category encompasses authors, poets, composers, architects, painters, sculptors, and movie directors. Performing artists are typically singers and actors, and we will look more closely at them in the section about celebrities later in this chapter.

Historically, there are two groups of creative artists that have pioneered changes in styles: painters and sculptors. Art historians have amply documented the individuals who made up the avant-garde in different artistic developments. For many of the artistic developments that have taken place since the Renaissance, the pattern has been that they first emerged in the visual arts and then crossed over to literature and music. This is shown in Figure 2.1.

Whether we are discussing romanticism, impressionism, expressionism, or any other "ism," by and large, painters have been the first to express new artistic ideas or moods because the cost of

Style	Impressionism	Expressionism	Modernism	Minimalism
Genres	Themes: dreams, nature, man governed by his instincts	Themes: inner life, psychoanalysis	Themes: machines, technology, the metropolis, speed	Themes: modern impersonal life, big city anonymity
Art	**1874** Claude Monet	**1893** Edvard Munch	**1907** Georges Braque, Pablo Picasso	**1963** Donald Judd
Music	**1892** Claude Debussy	**1909** Arnold Schönberg	**1913** Igor Stravinsky	**1964** Steve Reich, Philip Glass
Literature	**1901** Thomas Mann	**1912** Franz Kafka	**1922** James Joyce	**1967** Raymond Carver

The year given is the year in which the artist had a breakthrough with a new style (ism) in the genre.

Figure 2.1 Trend-creating artists since 1874

producing a painting is often lower than the cost of producing other artistic products. Traditionally, a composer of operas and symphonies often needed a whole orchestra to perform his music, entailing considerable costs. An author needs a publisher to get his book published. A movie director must assemble substantial human and financial resources to create his work. However, a canvas, paint, and brushes are all it takes to produce a painting. Of course, this is not the same as claiming that the painters were the first ones to produce new thoughts and ideas, but they have been uniquely positioned to show their new style to the public quickly after they have created it.

Today, production methods in many of the arts have changed dramatically thanks to new technologies. Now it is possible for almost anyone to publish a book or music on the Internet. That artists create trends in art is nothing new, but what is worth paying attention to (once again) is that people who are creative are often also trendsetters in areas other than their own.

In the 1950s, the black understated style of the beatniks and the existentialists (to whom we will be introduced further in Chapter 4) first became popular attire. Two women, Joyce Johnson and Hettie Jones, both living in Greenwich Village in New York City, were close to several of the beat writers (intimately, in some cases) in the early 1950s. They both wore polonecks and dancers' tights bought in a local store. These soon became typical of the beatnik style for women, but it would be nearly a decade before tights were mass-produced for all women. By then the beatnik way of dressing had been popularized in the media, notably in the musical *Funny Face* starring Audrey Hepburn. When this popularization happened, the artists and their girlfriends reacted by changing their style. They started thrift shop dressing, decorating dresses with beads themselves and wearing embroidered shawls, which became hallmarks of hippie style in the late 1960s and early 1970s.

WEALTHY PEOPLE

In Chapter 1 there was another clue that we should look into: we learned that people are more preoccupied with style and taste when they are well-off because then they are at the top of the Hierarchy of Needs. Wealthy people live their lives at the top of Maslow's Hierarchy of Needs with a focus on the aesthetic side of living.

Aristocrats and other wealthy people have long used their wealth to decorate almost everything with which they came into contact. They could afford to pay attention to their clothes, and they had different outfits for different occasions—something that is common today. An example of the wealthy creating and setting trends in the late nineteenth century was a young man named Griswold Lorillard. In 1886 he and some of his friends came to the annual ball of the elite Tuxedo Club in his hometown of Tuxedo Park, New York. All the young men of his set came to the ball wearing tailless dress jackets, having had the tails of the traditional full formal dress suit removed. Thus the tuxedo was born, and in fact has become a permanent fixture in clothing and apparently a rather permanent part of some people's style of living. However, as we shall see in the next chapters this is not the only and not the typical ending to a trend.

A twentieth-century example of the influence of the wealthy on style was Babe Paley. In the 1950s and 1960s, she was one of the most famous high-society women in the United States. She was married to the founder of CBS, William S. Paley, and became a close friend of the homosexual writer Truman Capote. She at one time topped the Best Dressed list and was also inducted into the Fashion Hall of Fame. According to biographer David Grafton, "Women in all walks of life did their best to emulate not only her clothing but her bearing. . . . Once, as she emerged from a fashionable Manhattan restaurant and discovered that the weather had turned warmer, she removed the scarf from around her neck and unthinkingly tied it to her handbag. Naturally, the media flashbulbs were awaiting her, and soon this 'innovative fashion statement' was transmitted via the fashion press to the nethermost regions of the country. In no time, women throughout America were tying scarves to their handbags."

Ten years later Jacqueline Kennedy and her sister, Lee Radziwill, were tying scarves to their handbags.

A similar example from the mid-1990s comes from England. The then-22-year-old Jemima Khan had a status similar to that of Babe Paley's in the United States in the 1950s. The daughter of one of the wealthiest men in Great Britain, the late Sir James Goldsmith, she was a friend of Princess Diana and was married and later divorced from the Pakistani cricket player and politician Imran Khan. In 2001 she was honored with the British Fashion Award as the nation's best-dressed woman. In 1996, Jemima was photographed wearing a cardigan in a bohemian color mix with a velvet ribbon border. British *Vogue* reported that she had purchased the cardigan at a small store in West London named Voyage owned by two former hippies. In the spring of 1996, British *Elle* predicted that this "new bohemian" style would be big in the autumn. Shortly thereafter the style was labeled boho chic—short for bohemian chic.

Fashion designers began copying the boho chic style, making it a major trend at the end of the 1990s. As fashion journalist Brenda Polan wrote in the London *Daily Mail* in 2001: "Nearly five years on, [the style is] still feature[d] in chain stores and mail-order catalogues."

GAY MEN

From Chapter 1 we also have a clue about gay men as trendsetters. Before highlighting more examples it is worth noting that there are indicators that a key difference between men and women is that men—contrary to the common belief—generally are more visually and aesthetically minded than women, whereas women are more emotionally minded than men. Support for this theory is found in the fact that men mainly focus on looks when choosing a partner, whereas women give more weight to other qualities. The Kinsey Institute for Research in Sex has also documented that men more frequently than women focus on faces when looking for what is sexually attractive in a person of the opposite sex. Throughout evolution, the value males have placed on female beauty has made women pay more attention to *their* looks in order to make themselves more attractive to men.

This theory can help explain why some homosexual men are preoccupied with looks and style, both their own and their partner's. In the twentieth century, it was obvious that some—although far from all—gay men were more interested in aesthetics and their own looks than the average heterosexual man was. This may again help explain why there is an overrepresentation of gay men among trend creators and trendsetters in the evolution of modern lifestyle.

In the twenty-first century, the situation is changing, as more and more heterosexual men are also becoming interested in design and style. An article in the *Village Voice* entitled "Post-Straight: How Gay Men Are Remodeling Regular Guys," focused on the fact that more and more heterosexual men are imitating gay men in many aspects of style: "This process has been evident for years in big cities, where gay men are rewriting the rules of what it takes to be a real man. Glossy magazines have noticed that straight men are increasingly looking gay, but the influence is more than a matter of working out, waxing, and wearing Prada. It involves a profound change in consciousness . . . the gay sensibility is rubbing off on receptive straights."

The phenomenon of heterosexual men "gay-acting" got its own name with the term *metrosexual*: *metro* because the behavior is a big-city phenomenon, and *sexual* because homosexual men have been the trendsetters.

Surveys have indicated that homosexuals are often trendsetters in lifestyle consumption. One example of gay men as trendsetters is the case of Absolut vodka. In the early 1990s, Absolut was a lower-end, no-name vodka. The marketers of Absolut initially focused on the gay community in San Francisco, kicking off their promotion with a funky ad campaign in the gay media. As a result, gay men began to drink Absolut. This helped catapult Absolut to *the* top-selling vodka in the United States.

A survey of American consumers' early online consumption around 2000, carried out by the advertising agency Witeck-Combs in cooperation with Harris Interactive, showed that among gays and lesbians, 28 percent engaged in online bank transactions, whereas only 21 percent of heterosexuals did so. Among gays and lesbians, 26 percent had bought from online auction houses, whereas only 19 percent of heterosexuals had done so. The survey also showed that homosexuals were one of the most active groups of consumers on the Internet.

In 2005, another survey by Witeck-Combs and Harris Interactive showed that more gay men and lesbians than heterosexuals were interested in the then relatively new and innovative hybrid cars. The difference was considerable: 51 percent of gay men and lesbians and 34 percent of heterosexuals were interested in buying a hybrid car. There can be different reasons for this, but hybrids certainly do represent a new trend in cars.

Homosexual men—like the other groups highlighted in this chapter—are a very mixed group of people. The extent to which gay men are underrepresented in some professions is difficult to know, but there is no doubt that they are overrepresented in one profession: clothing designers (and related professions like makeup artists and stylists). Most of the most famous male fashion designers are gay. To name but a few gay designers who are also brand names: Giorgio Armani, Yves Saint Laurent, Tom Ford, Alexander McQueen, Karl Lagerfeld, John Galliano, Domenico Dolce and

Stefano Gabbana, Jean Paul Gaultier, Marc Jacobs, and the late Gianni Versace.

Gay men have played a significant part in trends that are related to style in the broad sense of the word. In 1992, the newsletter *Iconoculture* from the U.S. ad agency of the same name wrote: "Tattoos—once strictly a trademark of military service and Harley hogsters—are showing up across the socioeconomic scale." Tattoos originated as body decorating in Tahiti and the other island societies in the Pacific Ocean. For centuries, only sailors traveling to these islands got tattoos. Later the sailors themselves learned the technique, and it spread to other Far East cultures and then to Europe and America.

At first, getting a tattoo was something that only men in the military and prison inmates did. After World War II, bikers started getting tattoos. Some gay men were attracted to the biker culture and started imitating biker style. In his book *Dirty Pictures*, Micha Ramakers describes how tattoos started showing up in gay erotic drawings in the 1960s. In his autobiography, movie director Wakefield Poole writes about a popular gay porn model who got tattoos in the late 1960s. The fact that gay porn magazines were almost the only kind of printed material targeting gay men at the time made these magazines the equivalent of today's lifestyle magazines. In other words, many gay men were exposed to this porn model with tattoos and were inspired to get tattoos themselves in the 1970s. In the 1980s, tattoos became still more popular among gay men as a way of distancing themselves from the feminine image that many gay men had at that time. In the 1990s, tattoos had become an almost mainstream phenomenon among both gays and straights, men and women. *U.S. News & World Report* said in an article that tattooing ranked as the sixth fastest-growing retail venture of the 1990s, right behind the Internet, paging services, bagels, computers, and cellular phone service.

CELEBRITIES

Several celebrities have already been named in this chapter, and this group seems to be worth looking into also. Our current culture has an obsession with celebrities, and the influence of famous people is tremendous. People want to know all about them, to look like them, and to be like them—easily done given the high number of magazines chronicling the lives of famous people. Most celebrities are neither trend creators nor trendsetters, but that having been said, a celebrity can have a very powerful influence. How powerful that influence is will depend upon the celebrity's position in what I call the "celebrity hierarchy," the six levels of status of celebrities—given here with some random examples:

1. Icons: Madonna, David Bowie
2. Megastars: Puff Daddy, Jennifer Lopez
3. Superstars: Cher, Justin Timberlake
4. Stars: Chloë Sevigny, Lenny Kravitz
5. Minor celebrities: former contestants of *American Idol* and similar TV shows
6. Wannabes: reality TV-show participants

The icons are worshipped for decades and are known by many people, whereas the wannabes are often forgotten in less than 15 minutes. The status of a celebrity is very important in determining that celebrity's potential trendsetting influence. In general, the higher a celebrity is in the hierarchy, the more the celebrity can affect trends. But even a minor celebrity may have a huge influence on just one group or community—the gay community, for instance.

Madonna is at the very top of this celebrity hierarchy, which means that her influence on style and taste is enormous. In his memoir former U.S. Marine Corps officer Rich Merritt (who is gay) wrote about a friend of his in South Carolina: "Amber . . . styled her hair just like Madonna had in one of the Material Girl's darker looks of 1984."

Among Madonna's many contributions to modern pop culture is her book *Sex*, published in 1992. The book consisted of erotic photographs of Madonna; it was one of the most widely discussed popular books in 1992, and it inspired many advertising people throughout the 1990s. In the following years, ads became more and more sexually daring and broke several sexual taboos.

A growing number of celebrities now have their own fashion clothing or accessory collections. The American rapper Eve was one of the first to get her own clothing and accessory collection. She got the idea for her collection after a concert in Albany, New York, in 2000. When she was looking out at the audience of thousands of young girls, she noticed that they were dressed like her. At that time she had been modeling in ad campaigns for Tommy Hilfiger and Sprite. After the concert, she thought: "What am I doing modeling other people's clothes?" She started designing clothes that she liked, and three years later the first Fetish collection was introduced and sold in major U.S. department stores.

OTHER STYLE-CONSCIOUS SUBCULTURES

Throughout the entire twentieth century, we saw the development of more and more subcultures. In some cases the term *subculture* is assumed to refer to groups of people who are "underground" or "obscure," representing either just a very small group or one that is extremely different from mainstream culture. In reality, all the groups mentioned so far could be called subcultures, as none of them represent any kind of majority. But they are for different reasons preoccupied with style and taste. There are several more groups that are also preoccupied with style and taste, and they often also get to influence mainstream culture, both as trend creators and as trendsetters. Who these "other style-conscious groups" are will often change over time. But three examples are bodybuilders, drag queens, and chefs.

Bodybuilding was a fringe activity within the sports world for most of the twentieth century. After World War II, it became a hobby of some men, many of whom were gay. The writer Edmund White, who is gay, writes in his autobiography that in the 1960s, "American gays, at least New Yorkers, were already beginning to work out."

In 1967, Austrian-born bodybuilder Arnold Schwarzenegger became Mr. Universe—a title he won five times. He and the sport got a lot of media attention, and in the 1970s bodybuilding became increasingly popular. In the 1980s more gyms opened, and by the 1990s a whole new fitness industry had been established. At the beginning of the twenty-first century, around 13 percent of adult Americans were members of a gym. Bodybuilders have also been influential in other aspects of male grooming, for instance, in the popularizing of shaving different parts of the body.

In the 1980s there was a well-established subculture of drag queens in New York City. The subculture involved mostly black and Hispanic young men who lived in poverty by day and played dress-up by night. Many of these men dressed as glamorous women, but some men who were effeminate by day chose to dress up as military officers, business executives, and other symbols of affluent, heterosexual America. There were regular contests, not just to determine who was the best dresser, but also who was best at dancing. One particular dance form was "voguing," a stylized dance that imitates the poses that models perform in front of the camera. In the 1980s, voguers often struck their poses in Greenwich Village's Washington Square Park.

In 1990 Madonna released her album *I'm Breathless*. The album included the song "Vogue," written and produced with

Shep Pettibone. "Vogue" was the first single release from the album and became Madonna's eighth U.S. number one hit. Madonna made a much-talked-about video of "Vogue" the same year, and she performed the song live at the 1990 MTV Music Awards. Madonna's song and video made voguing a popular dance concept in many parts of the world. Though few could do the moves, many became aware of the dance. Madonna did not create the trend; her role was, once again, that of trendsetter.

One gastronomic trend creator is the American chef Jeremiah Tower. In 1971 he started working as a chef at the then-unknown San Francisco Bay area restaurant Chez Panisse, founded and owned by Alice Waters. At the time, fine dining was dominated by French cuisine. With Alice Waters, Jeremiah Tower set out to create "serious simplicity" in food, using fresh, local ingredients. Eventually he became known as the innovator of modern American cooking and became one of the most influential chefs of the last third of the twentieth century.

In his autobiography, *California Dish: What I Saw (and Cooked) at the American Culinary Revolution*, he tells the story of the international culinary revolution that he created. In the spring of 1983, Tower (who besides being an artist in the kitchen is also gay) was hired by the Ocean Spray company to boost the role of cranberries in American cooking. Tower's assignment was to make a California lunch using cranberries. His main course was rack of lamb with a cranberry marinade, but first the journalists were served a snack of grilled sausages. "A hundred food journalists took one look . . . and one bite of sausage, raised their eyebrows with expectation, and away we went: salsa, grilling, and California were suddenly *it*," as Tower writes in *California Dish*. Over the next 20 years, California cuisine became a worldwide concept, and the use of cranberries in food preparation became commonplace, not only in the United States, but also in Europe and on other continents. In 2007, Danish supermarkets introduced a new type of "all-natural candy." The content? Dried organic cranberries.

MINGLING, OBSERVING, AND IMITATING

Trend creators are a very heterogeneous and extremely small group that includes people from all walks of life. Trendsetters, on the other hand, are a much larger group of people, and they are also a mixed group, but as we have seen in this chapter, there is an overrepresentation in certain groups. However, not everybody in these groups is a trendsetter. Most young people, artists, and gay men, for example, are part of the mainstream. In other words, these groups also have close ties to the mainstream. They are certainly not separate from the rest of society, which is important for the spread of a trend.

For the most part, human beings seem to prefer to socialize with people who, broadly speaking, share the same lifestyle. Trendsetters certainly prefer to socialize with other trendsetters, and because trendsetters have very different backgrounds, they actually end up mingling with a very diverse mix of people. This is important because it means that the groups we have identified as having an overrepresentation of trendsetters are not as separate socially as one might think. They interact and mingle in many different ways and in many different social settings. This means that people do not have to know one another or talk to one another in order to find out what is new. They can just observe.

Some common mingling spots for many trendsetters are theaters, concerts, art and design auctions, gallery openings, art exhibitions, charity events, award shows, festivals, and industry events such as fashion fairs. When trendsetters from different groups mingle, they get the chance to observe other people, get inspiration from them, and imitate them.

Changes in style and taste take time to spread widely; it is not something that happens overnight. A fashion fad may arise quite quickly in certain circles, but it will be limited to a small circle. The spreading of a new and innovative style to the *majority* of the people is a very complex process. One important point is that this process is most likely to happen when what I call *polysocial* groups are involved. Polysocial groups have many social contacts with other groups that differ from themselves. In our culture, most groups of people are actually *monosocial*: people who mostly interact with others very much like themselves. Trends rarely spread from monosocial groups.

If we look at how the trendsetting polysocial groups mingle in private, semipublic, and public settings, we see how trendsetters can observe other trendsetters and get the chance to get news of innovative styles and imitate them. Because polysocial groups mix in many ways, the innovations are observed and imitated by many different trendsetting groups. Here are some examples of polysocial mixes:

- Wealthy people can afford to use interior designers—and the majority of male interior designers are gay.
- Celebrities are often wealthier than the average person—and therefore associate with other wealthy people.
- Celebrities also enjoy being among people who will not treat them like idols, but can relate to the particulars of fame—creative artists, for example.
- Gay men are into style and design—and they mingle with women who are also into style and design. For instance, Madonna has said: "I've always had an affinity with gay men."
- Designers have a tradition of watching what goes on in youth cultures.
- In the social and sexual circles of gay men, there is more mingling of people with different incomes and social status than there is in heterosexual social circles.

This last point has, for instance, been documented by anthropologist Esther Newton in her study of the gay communities on

Fire Island, off the Long Island coast in New York State. Here there is "the A group, the wealthy . . . , the distinguished and the gorgeous, the young men flexing gym bodies and wearing the latest clothing styles. . . . Such trendsetters were magnets for young, good-looking and ambitious gay men."

This kind of mixing of groups with an overrepresentation of trendsetters is rather unique, but the important thing is that it does take place. To document the strong appeal of mingling for the trendsetting groups, one need only read the biographies and autobiographies of people belonging to these groups.

In a biography of fashion designer Calvin Klein, a number of parties with guest lists that included other designers, business moguls, socialites, artists (for instance, Andy Warhol), and celebrities (at one time actor Rock Hudson and his male lover) are described.

In Patricia Morrisroe's biography of gay photographer Robert Mapplethorpe, there are also several examples of how artists, wealthy people, subcultures, celebrities, and designers mix. In one instance, the New York City artist had traveled to San Francisco to attend an opening of a show of his risqué photographs. He was introduced to several wealthy society ladies. One of them who was "San Francisco royalty" ended up asking Mapplethorpe to escort her to a charity benefit during his stay. At another time, when Mapplethorpe was in Paris, he was introduced to gay fashion designer Yves Saint Laurent and many people in the designer's social circle.

In the early 1970s, Max's Kansas City was a trendy restaurant-bar-discotheque in New York City that was a good example of a typical venue for the clustering of trendsetting groups. In his book *POPism*, Andy Warhol wrote about Max's Kansas City: "Max's was the exact place where Pop art met Pop life . . . everybody went to Max's and everything got homogenized there." The restaurant attracted an amazingly diverse group of people—celebrities such as Mick Jagger, Jane Fonda, Bob Dylan, Jim Morrison, and Warren Beatty; politicians; Manhattan socialites; photographers; models; hairdressers; Hells Angels; drag queens; artists such as painter Robert Rauschenberg; and punk rock singer Patti Smith.

There have been and are many places like Max's Kansas City where this kind of mingling takes place. It was what happened at the most famous discotheque the world has ever known—Studio 54 in New York City. Studio 54 existed for only a few years in the late 1970s, but it was a playground for gay men, socialites, designers, artists, celebrities, and models.

A typical example of mingling in private could be designer Hedi Slimane, who is friends with people like chief curator Klaus Biesenbach from New York, filmmaker Gus Van Sant, Pet Shop Boys singer Neil Tennant, Sex Pistols manager and punk pioneer Malcolm McLaren, fellow designers John Galliano and Karl Lagerfeld, David Bowie, Boy George, *Visionaire* magazine editor Stephen Gan, Los Angeles–based artist Doug Atkins, and the late writer Susan Sontag.

Another example could be soccer player David Beckham and his wife, Victoria, who are friends with Elton John and his husband, David Furniss. In the memoir *My World* he tells about socializing with many other gay friends, with other celebrities, and with designers.

The connectedness and overlap between the polysocial groups is highlighted in Figure 2.2 in an oversimplified way—in reality, the trendsetting groups are also connected and overlap in all directions. The figure shows how the trendsetting groups spread out into mainstream society in all directions, metaphorically like a multipointed star. The "points" or "jags" reach out into the wider society and represent people who mingle with both the trendsetters and wider social circles in mainstream society. Though nonverbal communication plays an extremely important role in the

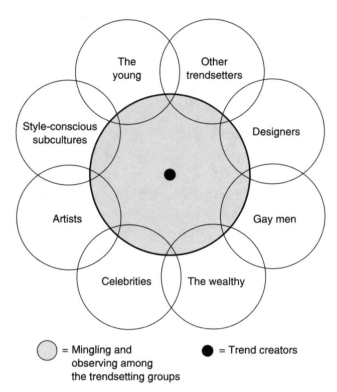

Figure 2.2 The trendsetting groups' relation to mainstream society

trend process, word-of-mouth communication and writing letters, postcards, and e-mails are also obvious parts of the communication among trendsetters and in their communication with the mainstream.

Figure 2.2 illustrates that there are other trendsetters outside the seven groups specifically named in the figure, but how they interact with mainstream society is not illustrated. (Note that there is no actual hierarchy among the groups in the figure and that the figure does not represent the actual sizes of the groups or their sizes relative to one another.)

TREND-SPOTTING CLUES

When we want to spot new and emerging trends, we can learn from the trend characteristics that have been explored in this chapter:

- Trend creators and trendsetters are often, but not exclusively, found in the same visually conscious groups.
- There is an overrepresentation of trendsetters in the following groups:
  - The young
  - Designers
  - Artists
  - Wealthy people
  - Celebrities
  - Gay men
  - Style-conscious subcultures
- If one or more of these groups accepts a new style, it is more likely to become a trend.
- The more trendsetters in each of these groups that adopt an emerging style, the more likely it is that it will become a trend.
- Trends that emerge among these trendsetting groups are likely to follow the same pattern as previous trends that have emerged from the groups.
- By studying the style and taste of the trendsetters, you can stay ahead of new developments in many different lifestyle areas.

3

WHAT'S THE
MOTIVE?

PSYCHOLOGY AT WORK

9 723456 485247

Singer and style icon Madonna is a typical trendsetter. In the 2005 movie about Madonna, *I Am Going to Tell You a Secret*, viewers can clearly see that she is part of several polysocial groups, both professionally and privately. Madonna is herself a wealthy artist and celebrity, but that is not *why* she is a trendsetter. To find the answer to what makes a person a trendsetter, we have to look at what motivates Madonna and other trendsetters.

Trendsetters seem to have some rather distinct personality traits in common. One of the most important is that they are curious and unafraid to stand out. Madonna has described herself in a television interview like this: "I'm a naturally curious person. . . . I don't want to repeat the same music. I don't like to do the same anything. . . . There are certain people in my life that I continue to work with again and again but we always try to do different things, explore different things. . . . I work best with people who are also not afraid to take risks. And once that person does not want to take risks anymore then I have to find someone else to collaborate with."

She also told the interviewer that she was very inspired by her colleague David Bowie: "When I was growing up I was a huge fan of David Bowie's—he really influenced me in terms of the way he used image. The way he evolved and changed. He kept going through all these evolutions; he was like a chameleon. He was very experimental and took a lot of risks. On that level he truly inspired me."

Since her singing career took off at the beginning of the 1980s, Madonna has herself been a chameleon, presenting herself in a different way on each new album cover:

Year	Album	Look
1983	*Madonna*	80s glamour
1984	*Like a Virgin*	New Romantics look
1986	*True Blue*	Marilyn Monroe look-alike
1987	*You Can Dance*	Mexican diva
1989	*Like a Prayer*	Super-elegant grunge
1992	*Erotica*	Super-vamp
1994	*Bedtime Stories*	Pinup blonde
1995	*Something to Remember*	Sensual, relaxed, elegant model style
1998	*Ray of Light*	Spiritual, dark mystic
2000	*Music*	Rhinestone cowgirl
2002	"Die Another Day"	Hard-hitting kick-boxer (single)
2005	*Confessions on a Dancefloor*	1970s glamorous disco queen

Of course, the question arises whether it is Madonna who is the trendsetter or her stylists. Naturally Madonna has a stylist at her disposal to deal with the practical side of styling for CD covers, as well as a personal makeup artist. Adrianne Philips was the stylist for the *Music* CD and the promotion tour Drowned World Tour, and Tom Pécheux was the makeup artist for *Music*. However, both Philips and Pécheux were quoted in *W* and *Elle*, respectively, as saying that the styling ideas for the CD covers typically come from Madonna herself. To *Vogue*, Philips has said: "The most important thing to understand about Madonna—and the thing that people resist believing—is that the way she works is not premeditated at all. It's all about picking up on things that she responds to intuitively. And she has an incredible eye. My job is to bring it all to her and to edit it."

Six years later, Adrianne Philips said in another interview about Madonna: "She's quite fearless. She's always willing to try new things. She's never nostalgic. She doesn't like to repeat herself—she likes moving forward. Her style secret is to always take risks and have fun. Wear something because you like it, don't consider what other people might think."

British soccer player David Beckham is also an archetypical trendsetter. He was born in 1975 in a typical middle-class family. He started his career with the U.K.'s top soccer club, Manchester United, and then transferred to another of Europe's top soccer clubs, Real Madrid in Spain, and later to the Los Angeles Galaxy in the United States. He has been captain of the English national soccer team and is married to former Spice Girls singer Victoria Beckham. Beckham has been called a trendsetter and a style icon by numerous magazines and newspapers, including *Time* magazine. In the fanzine *David Beckham—His Life in Words and Pictures*, his mother is quoted as saying that as a teenager, he was never afraid of standing out because of his interest in clothing.

In Tokyo, stylist Tomoki Sukezane has his own television show and is a recognized trendsetter. Fashion designer Hedi Slimane (who made Dior Homme a success in the beginning of the twenty-first century) has said of Sukezane in an interview: "He has this incredible curiosity for what is coming."

Curiosity—a desire to explore—and courage in one's style are common among trendsetters. Both are aspects of a person's personality, so we have to consult the research in personality psychology to find out why trendsetters are the way they are.

There is certainly no doubt that trendsetters can come from many different backgrounds and can be found in all walks of life. A trendsetter can be an artist—or a waiter, a retailer, or an office worker. Trendsetters may be gay, but most are not. They can be poor or rich. They can be 18 or 58 years old. Although, as we saw in the last chapter, a larger proportion of people in certain groups is at the cutting edge, ultimately, what makes a person a trend-setter has nothing to do with that person's career, sexuality, income, or age. What makes people "instinctively" like the same style and share the same taste is their personality, paired with a strong visual sense. Just because you have a low income does not mean that you cannot have a trendsetter personality, even if you may not be able to afford trendy new products.

SIX ATTITUDES TOWARD TRENDS

We now have an impression of who the trendsetters are and how they mingle with and observe one another. But how do they fit in with the rest of the population and ultimately determine the life of a trend? This process also has a pattern, which can best be visualized with a graphic model, the Diamond-Shaped Trend Model. This model, as illustrated in Figure 3.1, is a simplified way of representing an extremely complex process.

This model consists first and foremost of six different personality profiles:

- Trendsetters
- Trend followers
- Early mainstreamers
- Mainstreamers
- Late mainstreamers
- Conservatives

These six profiles can also be called trend groups—*groups* in order to stress that there are in fact many people with the same profile, and *trend groups* in order to stress that *all* people are part of trend processes. The Diamond-Shaped Trend Model thus in principle can represent the entire population, but as we shall see

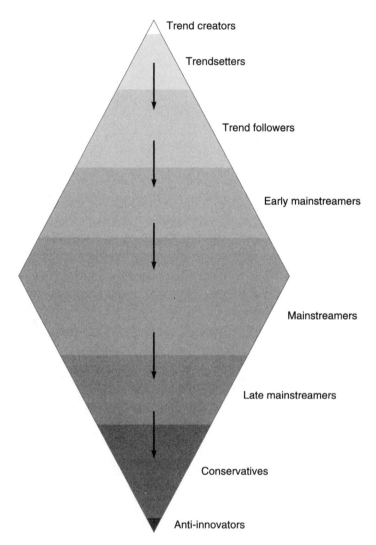

Figure 3.1 The Diamond-Shaped Trend Model

later in this chapter, specific trends do not necessarily affect the entire population.

As we have seen, there are some people—the trend creators—who are extremely innovative and inventive. This group of trend creators is very small, but it plays an important role in the trend process because it is these people who create the new styles and tastes that the trendsetters want to adopt. Even though trend creators are not a homogeneous group and cannot be said to represent a market, they are placed at the very top of the model because they are responsible for creating or doing something that can offset a trend.

There are also groups that do not accept changes at all—most notably groups such as the Amish in the United States. Their way of living has changed little since the 1700s—they still drive horse-drawn carriages, and their style of dress has barely changed in 250 years. There are also other individuals who oppose innovation, but these groups combined are not very significant and obviously do not constitute a market for modern lifestyle products. Even so, to make the model as realistic as possible, both of these profiles are included in the model:

- Trend creators
- Trendsetters
- Trend followers
- Early mainstreamers
- Mainstreamers
- Late mainstreamers
- Conservatives
- Anti-innovators

I developed this model in the mid-1990s in a research project aimed at finding out exactly how many different attitudes toward fashion and style there typically are. The many different fashion magazines and the highly differentiated fashion market make it apparent that people actually have a variety of attitudes toward fashion and style. Some (the trendsetters) will adopt new styles immediately, and others will only do so reluctantly.

One style I tracked began in the mid-1990s. The autumn and winter collections for 1996 trendy brands such as Prada and Miu Miu introduced gray as the new color, partly inspired by English school uniforms. The collections were—as always—presented to the fashion press and to buyers from department stores about six months ahead of the actual season. The following season, gray was also a very important part of the collections of designers such as Calvin Klein, Ralph Lauren, Gianni Versace, and Celine. Because of the trendsetting status of Prada and Miu Miu in the media, the rest of the fashion industry was inspired by these brands, and gray became the big new color in fashion in 1997 and 1998. Gray simply dominated all kinds of collections at all price points at the end of the 1990s. As the *New York Times* later wrote: "In the fall of 1998, . . . women were besieged with gray."

Gray had become popular in a short time, and by 1997 it was no longer the preferred color of the trendsetters. They wanted something completely different. In the spring of 1997, one could buy much more colorful clothing in the trendy stores. For instance, at the trendsetting fashion store New York Style Exchange (NYSE) in Los Angeles, you could buy three-quarter-length burgundy and floral-patterned satin pants. Gucci made a major comeback in the mid-1990s, introducing a more colorful look in its collections in 1997. In England, the London store Voyage introduced its bohemian and deluxe hippie style, which was discussed in Chapter 2. Clearly, while the mainstream was still wearing gray, the trendsetters were into colorful floral patterns. The most conservative women were—as usual—wearing dark blue. Then two years later the colorful patterns were becoming mainstream.

Early in my research, I started hypothesizing that there are eight distinct trend profiles or trend groups, and I decided to conduct an informal survey. Using photo collages, I constructed eight different trend profiles based on my analysis of the fashion market, which included the color gray, floral and bohemian patterns, and dark classic colors such as navy blue. In my mind, the bohemian style was very trend-oriented at that time, gray was mainstream, and navy blue was conservative.

In order to test the hypothesis, I chose 30 women and asked them to indicate which of the eight photo collages best represented their clothing style when they were out in public engaged in leisure activities (work clothing was not relevant because a woman may be required to wear a particular style, such as a conservative suit or a uniform at work).

Women who liked the mainstream and conservative styles had no problem choosing one photo collage that represented their clothing style. However, many of the most trend-conscious women chose two different collages to represent their style—that is, either the styles displayed in the photo collages were similar or they preferred to dress in both styles.

In order to refine the results of the survey, I decided to reduce the number of photo collages and trend groups to six. This seemed likely to make the differences between the trend groups more distinct. In a test of these six trend groups, I chose another 30 women and asked them to state which of the six photo collages best represented their clothing style. With only six profiles available, most subjects felt that they were represented by just one of the collages. In addition, I found that many of the subjects would not have been able to find a photo representing their style if the number of styles had been reduced further.

With only six trend groups, it seemed easy enough to visualize the trend process in fashion in a graphic model arranged in a vertical flow. The individuals who preferred the colorful styles that were newest to the market were placed at the top, the individuals who preferred gray were placed in the middle, and the individuals who preferred dark blue were placed at the bottom. This made it easy to present the flow characterizing the trend process.

But what was the difference between the women at the top of this model and the women at the bottom? Why would some women choose one style over another? I had had a personal experience that shed light on this question when I worked as a journalist for various lifestyle magazines. Back then, I specialized in interviewing many trendsetting designers, design students, artists, musicians, and regular trendsetters interested in interior design whose homes we were photographing. Most people I interviewed were, in my view, cutting-edge—that was what made them interesting to the magazines I worked for, and that was why I chose to interview them. Like Madonna, Beckham, and Tomoki Sukezane, they were all very curious about everything that was new and open to fresh influences in their lives.

Some of the statements I recorded as a journalist resembled the spontaneous statements given in connection with the two small surveys just mentioned, such as the following:

- "New styles are important."
- "I quickly get tired of my clothing."
- "I am very open to new fashion."
- "I will never be the first to wear that kind of clothing."
- "I dislike changes in fashion."

The survey showed that the subjects who preferred colorful and patterned clothing talked about how much they liked changes in styles, whereas the test subjects who preferred dark blue clothing stated that they did not like style or fashion changes (at least not in relation to what *they* were wearing). Many of the women tested who had a preference for the colorful style indicated that a couple of years back they had been into gray. The ones who preferred dark blue seemed to have liked that color for many years and preferred not to alter their wardrobes, at least not very much.

It appeared that the key differences among the six profiles had to do with the individuals' willingness to change, with their openness as consumers to new styles. The trendsetters—positioned at the top—liked changes in style and fashion, whereas the people positioned at the bottom were unwilling to make changes and sometimes were even hostile toward changes in style and fashion.

This insight led to my conclusion that the vertical dimension of the graphic model is willingness to change at the top and unwillingness to change at the bottom. In the upper half, there is openness to new styles; in the bottom half, there is a dominant desire for the familiar when it comes to style.

GROUP PSYCHOLOGY

People have many different attitudes toward changes in style and taste. Madonna and Beckham are at one end of the spectrum; Amish people are at the other. Being a trendsetter can be explained by a certain psychological profile, and therefore it makes sense to consult psychological literature, in particular research on personality, to find an explanation for the existence of the different trend groups.

Some psychologists describe the human personality using a framework called the Big Five Personality Factors. A human being's personality can be described or measured using five different trait dimensions: Emotional Stability, Extraversion, Openness, Agreeableness, and Conscientiousness. Each of these five trait dimensions has several subdivisions. Each human being has a unique combination of the Big Five trait dimensions. If we look at the trait dimension Openness, we find three subdimensions, with the terms that seem to characterize trendsetters to the left:

Imaginative...Practical
Preference for variety.................................Preference for routine
Independent..Conforming

Imagination, preference for variety, and independence can, of course, be expressed in connection with many different things: other human beings, cultures, experiences, styles, and products, to name a few. Some people like variety in the form of change; others have the opposite preference. Some people are independent in their style and taste; others are more conforming. Some people also use their imaginations in relation to style and taste; others do not.

The trendsetter psyche is probably more complex than just being open to new styles and tastes. A strong sense of individualism and a need to be different also play a part in the motivation of trendsetters. Think back to our discussion of psychologist Abraham Maslow in Chapter 1. He wrote that human beings get more individualistic when they reach the top of the Hierarchy of Needs. The strong sense of individualism that is present in Western societies in the twenty-first century can help explain the acceleration of fads and trends that took place during the twentieth century. In other words, when basic needs are met, people have more freedom to focus on style and taste to express *their* individualism.

Individualism can, of course, be expressed in many ways; the preference for variety is only a small part of the trendsetter overall personality, but it plays an important role in understanding trends.

To understand the trend groups' different preferences for variety and the opposite, the dimension line *Preference for variety–Preference for routine* can be divided into six sections (one for each trend group). In one survey, I asked men and women between the ages of 20 and 60 to measure their openness to new styles by placing themselves in one of the six sections: "If you were to state how open you are to new, innovative styles, where would you place yourself on this line? The sections to the right represent the greatest openness to new products; the sections to the left represent the least openness to new products."

This and similar tests have made it possible to conclude that there was no relationship between earning a lot of money and having a preference for variety and to profile each of the six trend groups in more detail:

- *Trendsetters.* The trendsetters are the most open and curious individuals with regard to style and taste. They accept the idea that styles change, and they feel that change is a positive thing when it takes place at regular intervals. They are enthusiastic about innovative new styles, and they are the very first to adopt them. The trendsetters are those who dare to adopt a new, innovative style before it has been sanctioned by other people.
- *Trend followers.* The trend followers are a bit like the trendsetters, but they need to have seen other people use the innovative new styles before they themselves will use them. They are very open to style and/or taste changes, but they want to be sure they choose something that is about to be accepted. The trend followers get their inspiration from the trendsetters. The trend followers are, in turn, inspirational models for mainstreamers.
- *Early mainstreamers.* Early mainstreamers accept new styles just before the majority—before the styles become completely mainstream. A member of this trend group is more open to new styles than the average person but a little bit more hesitant than the trend follower. The trend followers need to have seen only a few people buy or use an innovative style, but the early

mainstreamers need to have seen a number of people wearing or using the style before they adopt it. In other words, they need to have seen both the trendsetters and the trend followers adopting the style.

- *Mainstreamers.* Mainstreamers are average in their acceptance of new, innovative styles. They buy or use a style because "everybody" seems to be doing so. They mimic the early mainstreamers in that they want what is tested and recognizable. People in this trend group do not want to be as trendy as the trendsetters, but they do not want to be seen as conservative either. Their motto could be: "Don't be the first to try the new, and don't be the last to drop the old."

- *Late mainstreamers.* Individuals in this trend group are very hesitant about and in some cases dismissive of changes in style and taste. They do accept the idea that style and/or taste have to change eventually. However, when they want to buy something new—something that was new several seasons ago—it is generally because they cannot get the style they are used to. Late mainstreamers are also aware that they may find themselves standing out from the majority by not accepting style changes at all. This is not desirable for this trend group in the long run.

- *Conservatives.* Conservatives prefer styles that have existed for years or even decades. They are the people who are the most skeptical of new styles. Conservatives do not like big changes in style and taste; in fact, they do not want any changes in style and taste—in any way. They are very happy with what they like. They will surrender to something new only when they cannot get the products that they know and have used for many years.

We now know that it is people who create trends. When we want to know why new trends emerge, the answer is simply that the trendsetters' motive, so to speak, is a craving for change and variation. They thrive on variation. Trendsetters only have to see a new style once in order to get hooked, whereas mainstreamers have to make the same observation thousands of times before they get onboard.

A LITTLE VARIETY, PLEASE

In Chapter 2 we met groups that were overrepresented among trendsetters. And now we see that some of the individuals in these groups have the same psychological profile. To further understand these groups, it's important to explore if there are other aspects in their personalities that makes them more open. Let's have a look at each group:

- *The young*. Young people are in a phase of their life where they are exploring their own identity, and their personality has not yet become fully established. Thus, it seems likely that young people, who are generally more open-minded than the population as a whole, are considerably overrepresented among trendsetters.
- *Designers*. In order to thrive in their profession, designers must be interested in creating something new because this is often the focus of design. There is no doubt that designers are more imaginative than the general population. And more designers have traditionally worked freelance than the rest of the population, indicating that they like variation in their work.
- *Artists*. As a group, artists also are more creative and imaginative than the general population. Though they are a very diverse group, there are many examples of artists who have changed their artistic style during their career, thus showing a preference for variety, indicating more risk taking. Also, being an artist means risking not having a permanent income.
- *Wealthy people*. Some people are born rich; others make their fortunes in their own lifetimes. There is no doubt that wealthy people are a very diverse group who psychologically may be representative of the general population. Therefore, it is debatable

whether there is an overrepresentation of people who are open to variance and change in this group. But wealthy people who are trendsetters are the ones who can best afford the most expensive new styles; therefore, this group plays an important role in the trend process.

- *Celebrities.* Performing artists as a whole are more creative than the general population. They also tend to have more nonpermanent employment. When the careers of performing artists are judged by critics, those critics often focus on the artists' artistic growth, which further reflects the need for performing artists to be comfortable with change and variety.

- *Gay men.* Even though most gay men have the same highly different psychological profiles as the straight male population, at least some gay men are more emotional and empathetic than other men. People who have empathy probably have a better chance of appreciating variety, which may reflect their own preference for variety. And there is no doubt that there is a big overrepresentation of gay men among people who are interested in style and design, creating some overlap with the artist and designer categories.

- *Other style-conscious subcultures.* As described in Chapter 2, a style-conscious subculture is a small group of people who are in one way or another preoccupied with style and taste. When viewed as a whole, they naturally represent all kinds of psychological traits. Certainly not all style-conscious subcultures have an overrepresentation of people who are open to change; some people in these groups may be open to change, but others may just want to stick to an established style.

SIZING UP

Having established the six trend groups, the next step in developing the Diamond-Shaped Trend Model was to determine the size of each trend group. Based on how people placed themselves in the six sections in the survey, the six trend groups break down into the following percentages (rounded subjectively for each group):

- Trendsetters: 5 percent
- Trend followers: 10 percent
- Early mainstreamers: 20 percent
- Mainstreamers: 40 percent
- Late mainstreamers: 15 percent
- Conservatives: 10 percent

The trend creators and the anti-innovators are defined, respectively, as the 1 percent who are the most creative in coming up with new ideas and the 1 percent who are the least likely to buy anything new. With the Diamond-Shaped Trend Model, we can see that in the general population, about 5 percent can be characterized as trendsetters, but they are trendsetters in different areas. This is important: the Diamond-Shaped Trend Model should generally not be viewed as representing the entire population; it represents only the part of the population that for different reasons will be affected by the change. The Diamond-Shaped Trend Model is normally best used to represent only a specific group, for instance, people who are into gardening, or people who own cars or pets, or people who are decorating their homes for the first time. Among all these groups a trend will follow the flow in the Diamond-Shaped Trend Model.

The trend process starts when the different trend groups are inspired from the top of the model. The downward vertical orientation of the model was chosen primarily for aesthetic reasons. There is no implication of a social or other hierarchy in the model.

As mentioned, the model is, of course, a simplified representation of a complex process. But now we can define a trend as the process by which a style moves from trendsetters to mainstreamers. Once the style has become mainstream, the process going from mainstream to conservatives begins. This process does represent a change, but the trend is no longer growing, and it is quite predictable that interest in a certain product, design, or style will shrink or even vanish unless the original product, design, or style becomes part of a continuous product development (more on this in Chapter 5).

TRENDSETTERS FOR LIFE?

Keep in mind that, in general, in the Diamond-Shaped Trend Model it is the style that changes position, not the individual. This has to do with the fact that we have a stable core—our personality—that is not likely to change dramatically once it is fully developed. This is the conclusion of a number of studies in which scientists observed the same groups of people for several decades.

In one such study, psychologists Paul Costa and Robert McCrae from the National Institute on Aging in Baltimore studied several hundred men from the time they were about 25 years old until they retired. Based on the subjects' responses to a number of hypotheses and questions, they were placed in different categories: insecure, anxiety-prone, codependent, and so on. In one of their studies, Costa and McCrae concluded: "For the great majority of people, the self-concept at age 30 is a good guide to personality at age 80." The research has documented, for instance, that among adults, a person's openness is persistent.

It probably is correct to say that it is only when a person is past 30 years of age that his or her "true" trend personality kicks in. This could explain why some people who were, say, hippies, in their early 20s still dress like hippies three decades later. In reality they are not trendsetters but rather conservatives. Or, in some cases, they are in fact trend creators, not trendsetters. One of the differences between trend creators and trendsetters is that trend creators often stick for years to the style they created. This can explain why, as some of the original hip-hoppers aged, they stayed with the same style that they helped originate.

Few psychologists will conclude that no changes take place in personality over time for all people—the changes are just not very dramatic. Illness, such as depression, can have an enormous influence on one's personality, as can stressful situations such as unemployment, divorce, or the death of a close family member. But there is a difference between short-lived changes and fundamental and definitive changes in behavior and personality.

Being a trendsetter does not mean that you are governed *only* by your trendsetter personality. You are also governed by your financial situation, your needs and interests, your time constraints, and your values. And while it is rare to change personality after a certain age, a person can change values. Values play an important part in consumption behavior. If someone who is a trendsetter changes her values in a "sustainable" or "organic" way, this could make her buy "green" or "organic" products, even if they are not trendy in terms of style. Also basic needs take precedence over personality type with regard to shopping, so it certainly is possible to change behavior, if not personality. This will explain why someone who has been a trendsetter over time later may appear not to behave like one.

Looks change as we age and we get more life experience ("been there, done that"), and this will typically alter our needs but not our personality. When trendsetters age, they will buy products that are different from those they bought when they were young. For example, at age 30, a woman will be interested in new clothes; at 40, she will be interested in new clothes for her children; at 60, she will be interested in the new beauty products for "mature women"; and at 80, she will be interested in hearing aids in the most trendsetting design.

Trendsetters may be interested in and aware of a trend, and yet for various reasons not change their style. For instance, it is extremely rare to see trendsetters change their entire home décor because a new style of furniture and home design becomes trendy. They would like to, but unless they are wealthy, they will often focus on other needs and interests. To put it simply, when it comes to home decoration, only the trendsetters among those decorating a home for the first time will typically adopt a new style in interiors. They will then mostly affect other people who are also decorating a home for the first time at the time.

Trendsetters who earlier went through this process of decorating a home for the first time will typically not be part of this trend process because they will focus on others needs and interests. This explains why the interiors of many homes do not change over time. But if home decoration is a big personal interest or if money is not an issue, later in their lives trendsetters will also act as trend-setters in home decoration. Wealthy gay Italian movie director Count Luchino Visconti (whose family is from Milan) clearly had a trendsetter personality and the money to act on it, so in his case he could follow his inclinations even in home decoration.

In the 1930s, when Visconti was in his twenties, very few people knew of or could afford to buy bags and suitcases at a little shop named Louis Vuitton in Paris. But Visconti was one of its regular customers. In his biography of Visconti, Gaia Servadio writes: "[Visconti] would go and order scores of L.V. cases: he was almost their only customer. Visconti launched a fashion because, little by little, friends and admirers were seen everywhere carrying L.V. suitcases."

In the 1950s, Visconti once again proved to be a trendsetter. This time it was art nouveau, Liberty prints, and Jugendstil objects, including vases by Gallé and Lalique. Servadio writes: "By combing small markets for Art Nouveau objects, Visconti once again launched a fashion, copied first of all by his 'set' and then by others: the strength of Visconti's personality [was] demonstrated by his rediscovery of a trend, a painter or a style which was immediately copied, from the Louis Vuitton suitcases to the Lalique vase. . . . He was ahead of fashions . . . and, unwillingly, 'launched' whatever he touched."

In the early 1960s, when Visconti was in his fifties, he was still open to changes. "It was open house at Via Salaria and its décor changed as Visconti's taste changed," Servadio writes of this time in Visconti's life.

When Visconti died in 1976, inexpensive travel and worldwide communication had yet to make it possible for trends to spread globally as fast as they do today. In the mid-1970s, the still very exclusive Louis Vuitton leather goods store in Paris was unknown except to the wealthy people who could afford to shop there. The Louis Vuitton bags and suitcases were handmade by fine crafts-men, often to a customer's specific order. In the 1980s this changed as yuppies heard of the store and the fact that the client list was rumored to read like *Who's Who* and the *Almanach de Gotha*, the official peerage publication for the royal and aristo-cratic families of Europe. Yuppies from Europe, the United States, and Japan started shopping there. Sometimes there would be lines at the door and waiting lists for products. Realizing the potential, the owners of Louis Vuitton started opening more stores all over the world, underlining that the existence of stores—and thus the availability of products—plays an important part in trends.

TREND-SPOTTING CLUES

When we want to spot new and emerging trends, we can learn from the trend characteristics defined in this chapter:

- The trend process is a social process involving six different trend groups:
  - Trendsetters
  - Trend followers

- Early mainstreamers
- Mainstreamers
- Late mainstreamers
- Conservatives
- The trend process starts with the trendsetters and ends with the conservatives.
- By combining insight into what is happening among the trend-setters with knowledge about the trend process, it is possible to make a qualified prediction about future needs.

4

THE SETTING

WHERE WORLDWIDE
TRENDS BEGIN

9 723456 485247

As "trend detectives," we cannot avoid acquainting ourselves with the settings where trends have their source. We know now that trends emerge and grow in metropolitan areas with many polysocial groups, but can trends that influence people all over the world come from just any large metropolitan area? In this phase of our search for clues, we have to look for patterns in the national and global spread of trends. And a first lead could be to check out some of the settings that we have encountered already: Los Angeles, San Francisco, New York, Paris, London, Milan, and Tokyo.

LOS ANGELES

Los Angeles is the "nerve center" of southern California, and it was from southern California that one of the very first youth cultures spread across much of the Western world after World War II. It began when a group of former GIs and combat pilots began touring California on Harley-Davidson motorcycles. They were soldiers who felt restless after having been discharged and who had difficulty reinserting themselves into civilian society.

One U.S. Air Force squadron—the 303rd Bombardment Group, which had flown many missions into Germany and France—had been known as Hell's Angels. Back in civilian life, some of the squadron's former pilots formed a motorcycle club using a variation of that name. The first Hells Angels Motorcycle

Club was founded in 1948 in San Bernardino in southern California. The members of this club and all the Hells Angels clubs that followed dressed in a similar style, with an emphasis on wearing black Schott leather jackets. (The leather jackets came from the company that had supplied Air Force pilots with their leather bomber jackets.)

During the next few decades, Hells Angels Motorcycle Clubs were founded in other states and, by the 1960s, in Europe as well. The members generally joined the clubs in their late teens or early twenties. The biker lifestyle that grew out of the Hells Angels still thrives in many countries, inside and outside of motorcycle clubs.

For decades surfing also was the epitome of the California lifestyle. But historically, surfing started in Hawaii, where the Hawaiian people called surfing *heénalu*, which directly translated means "wave gliding." When the English Captain James Cook came to Hawaii in 1778, he noted in his diary that *heénalu* was "a most supreme pleasure." Later, when Christian missionaries came to the islands, surfing was declared a heathen pastime and was more or less banned.

When the writer Jack London, who lived in San Francisco, came to Hawaii in 1907 with his friends Alexander Hume Ford and George Freeth, they became avid surfers. Upon returning from their trip, they formed the world's first official surfing association, Outrigger Canoe and Surfboard Club. Jack London later depicted his adventures in his memoir *The Cruise of the Snark*. Upon his return from Hawaii, Freeth mounted surfing demonstrations in Redondo Beach near Los Angeles. Over the following decades, the sport became more and more popular along the California coast. One important figure in this process was a Hawaiian, Duke Kahanamoku. Born in 1890, he went on to be both a surfer and an Olympic swimmer, winning gold and silver medals at the Olympics in 1912, 1920, and 1924.

Between Olympics and after retiring from Olympic competition in 1924, he traveled in the United States and to Australia to give swimming and surfing exhibitions, thus popularizing the sport. His surfing exhibition in Sydney, Australia, in 1914 is considered a significant moment in the development of surfing in Australia because trendsetting Australians realized that the conditions in Australia were ideal for this new, exciting sport. For many years, while giving surfing exhibitions, Kahanamoku lived in Los Angeles.

Duke Kahanamoku preferred surfboards made of wood. But when the southern California surfer Hobie Alter developed a light plastic surfboard in the late 1950s, he transformed surfing into a modern lifestyle and an entire youth culture. The surfers developed their own dress code, with Hawaiian shirts, surf T-shirts with streetwise graphics, Bermuda shorts, surf trunks, and flip-flops. (The latter were inspired by the "zori" sandals worn by Japanese immigrants who labored in Hawaii's cane fields in the late 1800s.)

The first people to fully adopt surfing as a lifestyle was a group of rootless young people who lived near the beaches—the 1950s' beach bums. Their laid-back style became known and popularized through a number of movies with titles like *Beach Party* (1963), *Ride the Wild Surf* (1964), and *Beach Blanket Bingo* (1965). At the same time, bands like the Chantays, the Ventures, the Astronauts, Dick Dale & the Del-Tones, and not least the Beach Boys introduced a new music style: surf music.

California is not just about popular new sports and youth cultures. Los Angeles is the center of the American movie and television industry. No other city in the world has so many creative artists (directors, screenwriters, set designers) and performing artists (actors). These are genuinely polysocial groups. In his book *Behind the Screen*, William Mann has described the mingling that goes on in Hollywood. Already in the 1940s, most wardrobe designers and the majority of set decorators were openly gay men, and they had enormous influence on the style and taste being seen on movie screens all over the world. A former supervising set decorator with MGM told Mann that the 1934 movie *When Ladies Meet* "swept the nation" with an interest in early Americana, chintz, and ruffled organdy curtains.

Los Angeles is also home to many visual artists. This was documented in the Sunshine & Noir art show at the Armand Hammer Museum of Art and Cultural Center in Los Angeles. When the exhibition was touring in countries like Germany, Denmark, and Italy, *Forbes* magazine advised "cutting-edge collectors" to "head directly to Los Angeles . . . one of the world's hottest centers for new art." California also leads in car design, as many car manufacturers today have located design studios in southern California. One of the world's leading design schools for car design is the Art Center College of Design in Pasadena.

SAN FRANCISCO

The largest youth culture of the twentieth century emerged in northern California. They became known as hippies because they were hip, that is, they were "with it" and were informed about the latest ideas and styles. The roots of the hippie movement go back to the mid-1950s, when a small group of young writers and artists settled in San Francisco, the California coastal town of Carmel, and the nearby Big Sur area. They were called the beats.

Several writers had been living in Carmel and Big Sur since the beginning of the twentieth century, among them Henry Miller, who settled in Big Sur in 1947. While living there, Miller wrote a number of highly controversial erotic and autobiographical novels: *Sexus* (1945), *Plexus* (1949), and *Nexus* (1957). (Miller's books were banned in the United States and England for a long period.) But it was his earlier book *The Colossus of Maroussi* (1941) that many of the beats regarded as their founding text; this interest began to take shape as a "movement" in the 1950s. Among the original beats were Jack Kerouac, Neal Cassady, Allen Ginsberg, and William S. Burroughs (the latter two were later openly gay). The beats had a preference for working-class heroes, jazz, and Eastern spiritualism. It was Herbert Huncke, a friend of Allen Ginsberg, who used the word *beat* to describe how he felt disconnected from society. Jack Kerouac liked the word's suggestive tone of alienation, physical weariness, and the beatific. In 1948 he used the word in his novel *On the Road*, which became one of most innovative books of the 1950s with its breathless, ecstatic style (it was published in 1957).

William Burroughs became known for the psychedelic novels *Junkie* (1953) and *Naked Lunch* (1959). Both books were also considered highly innovative in their style and content.

When Ginsberg's *Howl and Other Poems* was published in 1957, its homoerotic themes were highly controversial. The police confiscated the entire printing at City Lights bookstore in San Francisco and arrested the owner, beat poet Lawrence Ferlinghetti, whose resulting trial ending in an acquittal was major news all over the United States. The trial made many young people aware that San Francisco was more open-minded than the rest of the country. Homosexual men began going to the city for vacations, and many later settled in the city, as had many gay sailors who did not want to go back to their hometowns after World War II. Today the city has one of the highest concentrations of gay men of any American city.

What had started in the 1950s as a small group of artists settling in the Bay Area had a considerable influence on the development of the hippie lifestyle and the youth revolution that started in San Francisco. "The mutation from Beat to hippie meant a switch . . . from a small group of writers and artists and jazz musicians to a mass youth movement. . . . The questioning of authority, the drugs, the experimental lifestyle, the leaning towards Eastern philosophy, all were carryover from the Beats," according to Ted Morgan in *Literary Outlaw: The Life and Times of William S. Burroughs.*

It almost goes without saying that the people living in San Francisco are a highly varied crowd. But what is important is that there are many people like Laura Pilz, who has lived in or near the Pacific Heights neighborhood in San Francisco since 1978. She is originally from a small town in Ohio. One of her neighbors, Jules Older, wrote this about her in a travel article about San Francisco: "In many ways, Laura is a typical San Franciscan and a typical Pacific Heightner: she's from somewhere else; she's smart, ambitious and succesful (she's a financial advisor); and she's unafraid of change."

People in California are quite different from one another, just as people who live in Illinois are. However, at the branch of the specialty food store chain Trader Joe's in Glenview, Illinois, the store manager was aware of one difference between Illinois and California: "We do lots of demos to give people an opportunity to taste and feel. . . . People here are more hesitant to try new things than in California where I'm from."

Apropos of taste, northern California is home to a large part of the American wine industry. It was here that the American wine awakening began in the mid-1960s when a visionary entrepreneur named Robert Mondavi founded his own winery. According to the book *Trading Up*, this "American revolution has catalyzed a global wine revolution. The United States, Australia, Chile, and South America are constantly innovating, raising quality at all price points, gaining market share, and making the American 'big' taste dominate worldwide."

The growth of California's cultural influence in the Western world is basically the result of two factors: celluloid and silicon. Silicon Valley in northern California plays a major part in the development of new technologies for electronic media. Nowhere else on the planet is there a greater concentration of companies in the information technologies. In southern California, Hollywood produces content for a variety of audiovisual media that are distributed around the globe, and the media (including Hollywood movies) play an extremely important role in any trend process.

The importance of silicon and celluloid does not mean that California's influence is limited to technology and media. It covers a lot more ground. Let's take furniture. In the early 1990s, furniture manufacturer Herman Miller in Michigan decided to introduce a new office chair that ended up being called the Aeron. The design of this chair was radically different from that of all other office chairs. This is how the design is explained on the company's Web site: "The transparency of the chair as a visual element was in keeping with the idea of transparent architecture and technology, which Aeron pioneered in advance of Apple's transparent iMac computers. Transparency is a major design movement."

When prototypes of the chair were being tested in Michigan in 1992, no one liked the minimalist design. (As mentioned in Chapter 1, minimalism was then an emerging trend in New York and Milan.) The testers liked sitting in the chair, but they thought it was hideous. However, even though the test evaluation came out unfavorably, Herman Miller needed a new product, and the Aeron was put into production. When sales of the product started, it looked as if the rest of the market agreed with the testers—except in two places. In Silicon Valley and in New York advertising agencies, people liked—and bought—the Aeron. The chair also won the design of the decade award from the Industrial Designers Society of America. It was used in Hollywood movies and in *Will & Grace*, a television sit-com about two gay friends and their female friends.

Through its adoption by trendsetters in San Francisco and New York, the Aeron became the best-selling chair ever manufactured by Herman Miller. And with that, it also became a widely copied chair.

NEW YORK CITY

For most of the twentieth century New York City was the world's most important cultural center. In art, musical theater, ballet, music, fashion, food, advertising, and many other areas, New York has been—and still is—extremely influential on a global scale.

In art, it was after World War II that American art began moving away from provincialism toward the avant-garde. The Whitney Museum in New York showed this by presenting a 1946 show with the title "Pioneers in the Modern Art of America," featuring the then avant-garde work of artists such as Joseph Stella, Charles Burchfield, and Georgia O'Keeffe. Today, New York probably has more painters and sculptors per capita than any other big city in the world. The city is also the number one location for selling art in the United States.

In the twentieth century, New York was also the fashion center of the United States. It is there that most of the best-known fashion designers have their offices, including Ralph Lauren, Calvin Klein, Donna Karan, and Marc Jacobs, to name a few.

For much of the twentieth century, New York probably was second only to San Francisco in terms of its percentage of gay men. The hippie style came out of San Francisco, but the style that was a reaction to the long-haired hippie style came out of New York. Male hippies had long hair whether they were straight or gay. But it was a group of gay hippies who were the first to cut their hair and get crew cuts. Among the first were movie director Wakefield Poole and his then boyfriend, Peter Fisk.

In his autobiography, Poole writes of a summer weekend in 1970 that he spent at the gay summer resort Fire Island Pines on the Long Island coast: "One weekend Peter and I decided to cut our hair with clippers. My hair was shoulder length, and I was ready for a change. I had been a hippie long enough. We had been trimming our body hair with dog clippers, so we decided to do our heads, cutting our hair shorter than a crew cut. Before the weekend was over most of the guys in the Pines had followed suit. People actually came to our house and asked to use our clippers."

The crew cut look spread to San Francisco and to other large American cities and later to large European cities. In the 1980s, long hair became completely unfashionable among men, gay or straight, in large cities and in small towns.

In most countries, homosexual men were stigmatized and per-secuted throughout the twentieth century. However, in the summer of 1969, a group of gay men, inspired in part by the civil rights movement, decided for the first time to fight police harass-ment. What later became known as "The Stonewall Riots" started one night in June 1969 when the police once again raided a popular gay bar called Stonewall. The fight against the harass-ment gave many homosexuals a new pride, resulting in more and more gays coming out of the closet. To many gay men at the time, having the opportunity to dance together became a symbol of freedom; until the riot, the police had routinely raided bars where gay men danced together.

Gay New Yorkers played a role in making a new dance culture popular during the period following "the Stonewall Riots." Even though the discotheque was a French invention, it was when this dance club phenomenon was imported to New York in 1962 that a whole new dance and music culture emerged—and evolved into the global phenomenon known as disco. The very first discotheques were clubs for heterosexuals, but early disco culture was predominantly a homosexual phenomenon born in mixed gay-straight clubs in New York City. Disco was a sharp break from the rock music that dominated the music scene at the time. Many of the first DJs playing disco were gay.

Light played an important role in disco culture. In the summer of 1970 at the gay discotheque the Ice Palace on Fire Island, an important new addition to the strobe lights and disco globe was introduced. A gay man who, according to the discotheque's founder, was "an electronic genius" took some old stereo systems, lightbulbs, and Christmas lights and invented lighting that pulsed with the music.

Disco culture grew from underground semipublic and public venues in the Greenwich Village and Hell's Kitchen areas of New York in the early 1970s to become completely mainstream in midtown Manhattan. In 1977, what would quickly become the world's most famous disco, Studio 54, opened in New York, and by then disco was becoming a worldwide phenomenon with an aesthetic of its own.

Studio 54 was well known for attracting an eclectic mix of people—gay and straight, rich and poor, celebrities and drag queens. One of Manhattan's first predominantly gay discotheques was the Sanctuary, which also had an eclectic mix of people. According to Jorge La Torre, who was a regular there in 1970, "There were people dressed in furs and diamonds, and there were the funkiest kids from the East Village. A lot of straight people thought it was the coolest place in town. . . . Women made up 25 percent of the crowd. . . . People came from all cultural backgrounds, from all walks of life." The Sanctuary was also racially mixed, which was rare at the time.

This mix of people made it possible for people to observe and imitate. One regular guest, Nathan Bush, told music historian Tim Lawrence: "We used to dress to go out. We didn't wear suits but we were always dressed. We didn't wear sneakers. That was unheard of. We wore shoes. . . . We would wear all of these clothes that were a step ahead of fashion. They were club clothes, and eventually straight men started to wear the same kind of thing."

A few years later, gay men started to dress down when going out. In 1972, a discotheque named the Tenth Floor opened. At the Sanctuary, people dressed up. That was not the case at the Tenth Floor. According to Tim Lawrence, "The regulars donned Levi's jeans, construction boots, a hooded zippered sweatshirt, and a waist-length flight jacket that was silver on the outside and orange on the inside, with the hood of the sweatshirt invariably flipped outside the jacket. . . . The Tenth Floor's neighbor made the flight jackets. . . . First the owners and staff wore them, then their friends wore them, and before you could mix two records together it was a trend. Bloomingdale's was selling them within a year."

In January 1978, Calvin Klein introduced his first menswear collection, which included "leather bomber jackets à la Christopher Street" (a then predominantly gay area in New York's Greenwich Village). At this time the style was also popular in many European cities.

In 1972, *Women's Wear Daily*, the fashion industry paper, wrote of a gay club that it was "making a big splash with the Firsties, those young New Yorkers who are the first anywhere. Just to be first." Gay men were officially labeled trendsetters.

A few years later, New Yorkers were again inventing a new music and dance style. While disco was going mainstream, a group of African American boys and men started what would become hip-hop culture (as mentioned in Chapter 2) and would eventually go global—not because New Yorkers travel all over the world, but because people from all over the world travel to New York. As Diane Von Furstenberg, the designer and president of the Council of Fashion Designers of America, has said: "Every designer of the entire world comes to New York to get inspired."

PARIS

There is no doubt that Paris has been home (and is home) to many artists and other bohemians. At the beginning of the nineteenth century, Europe's artistic center shifted from Rome to Paris. France and Paris have also played an important role in literature and movies. In the 1950s, Paris became a popular place to live for many American artists, including, among many others, the gay writer James Baldwin. The American expatriates mingled with existentialists in Left Bank cafés and jazz clubs. The cafés became the meeting place for intellectuals from all over the world. In the bars and cafés, philosophers, writers, actors, and musicians met. At the Café de Flore, the leading existentialist philosopher Jean-Paul Sartre, the writer Simone de Beauvoir, the singer Juliette Gréco, and the nouvelle vague movie directors held court. The existentialists wore black clothes. For men, the style was most notably a turtleneck sweater instead of the traditional shirt and tie. Women wore short skirts and a man's beret.

Because of their connections to African American jazz musicians, who in turn had contacts in Paris, one group of beats was inspired by the French existentialist philosophy and the minimalist black clothing style. This part of the beat movement became known as beatniks, and they popularized their style in the United States. Some of the beatnik writers and painters moved to Venice Beach near Santa Monica, west of Los Angeles. In 1956, the poet Stuart Perkoff settled there and opened the first café in the area. The dress code of the artists and the beats soon caught on outside the artistic community. Perkoff later remembered how "one morning we who lived in Venice woke up and walked out onto the Promenade and we saw hundreds of people who looked just like us."

For much of the twentieth century, Paris was regarded as *the* global center of fashion, fragrance, and food. The phenomenon of fashion was created in Paris by Charles Frederick Worth (as mentioned in Chapter 2). One of the best-known types of clothing to come out of Paris was the bikini. It was invented in 1946 by the French engineer and fashion designer Louis Réard. In the same year, the first person to wear the bikini was Micheline Bernardi, who wore it in a beauty contest in Paris. Another Frenchwoman, the actress Brigitte Bardot, wore a bikini in the 1956 movie *And God Created Woman,* which made not only Bardot but also the bikini famous internationally. A decade later wearing a bikini in some parts of the United States was not without problems. Meredith Hall writes in her memoir of growing up in the 1960s that up until 1965 you could get a citation for indeceny for wearing a bikini at the Hampton Beach in New Hampshire. She herself was one of the first girls at the beach to wear a bikini.

In the 1950s, a group of Paris fashion houses largely determined what was fashionable in Europe and North America. Paris was to fashion what the Vatican is to the Catholic Church. Apparel manufacturers and fashion magazines on both sides of the Atlantic looked to Paris for inspiration. Even beyond clothing, the Paris fashion houses had enormous influence. Fragrance became a major industry, which was dominated by France for most of the twentieth century after the Paris fashion houses introduced perfumes and lent them their names.

The writer Edmund White writes in his autobiography that when he was growing up in Ohio in the 1940s, "No one drank wine or used garlic or even ate in courses. . . . Travel to Europe was expensive and few people could afford it." But some Americans did go to Paris, and this would change both American eating and drinking habits. One of these Americans was Chuck Williams, the founder of the Williams-Sonoma chain of kitchenware stores. In 1952, this avid cook traveled to Paris, where he was introduced to French cooking equipment. Back home, he opened a specialty store for French cookware, presenting the merchandise in visually attractive ways just like in the stores in Paris. Today there are

Williams-Sonoma stores all over the United States, and they have effectively been part of the introduction of fine dining in the United States.

French chefs have had an enormous influence on cooking for centuries, but outside of France, this affected only elite society. French food started becoming an inspiration to "regular" restaurant chefs outside France in the late 1950s through young French chefs such as Paul Bocuse, Michel Guérard, and Alain Chapel. They invented a lighter, more relaxed food style that would later be called nouvelle cuisine. The nouvelle cuisine chefs replaced traditional heavy sauces with reductions of stocks and cooking liquids, and introduced small portions and visual presentation on oversized plates.

In 1962, another American went to Paris. His name was Robert Mondavi. In France, he studied the country's growing and winemaking methods. In his autobiography *Harvests of Joy*, he writes: "There was simply no significant market in America for fine wine at that time. While Italian families like ours ate and drank as our parents and ancestors had for centuries, we were the exception. For the vast majority, America was still a steak, potatoes, and beer kind of country." In 1966, Robert Mondavi founded his own winery in Napa Valley, California, and started laying the groundwork for the great interest in wine among a growing number of Americans.

Paris has had a certain appeal to many people for decades, but it has been especially appealing to those groups of people whom we have identified as being polysocial. The German homosexual novelist Klaus Mann wrote in his autobiography that Paris "was swarming with foreigners of all races, colours and social backgrounds." And as we shall see later in this chapter, having many international visitors plays a big part in taking a trend process from the local to the global because they go back or report home to tell about their observations.

LONDON

London has also had a huge influence on global style and taste, but, for instance, in fashion many of London's trend creators and trendsetters have not been professional fashion designers to the same extent as in Paris. In London, trendsetting has often been about young people creating "street fashion."

Even though London had a thriving youth and music culture after World War II, it was not until the mods (short for modernists) came on the scene that English youth culture really caught the world's attention. Mod style was partly inspired by the existentialists and beatnik style and included fitted jackets and trousers—the clothes the Beatles wore when they first became public figures. It was through their music that the style became popular in many different countries.

In England, the mod movement was also the beginning of what became known as "Swinging London." One of the best-known clothing styles to come of out of Swinging London was the miniskirt, officially created by Mary Quant in 1959. She had felt frustrated for many years because she could not find fashionable clothing that she liked, and therefore she began creating her own design. In 1968, Lynn Darling, then a 16-year-old girl, enrolled at Harvard University in Cambridge. Together with her friends she cut four inches off her skirts and turned them into miniskirts. Mary Quant is also credited with introducing, among other styles, go-go boots, shoulder bags, crocheted vests, and the 1960s girlie look (which was made famous by ultra-thin British top model Twiggy). These were all designs that became part of the Swinging London style.

In the mid-1960s, a group of working-class mods rebelled against a commercialization of the mod style by dressing in a completely different way. They chose to dress in a raw, aggressive, working-class-inspired clothing style: fitted blue jeans, suspenders, Doc Martens boots—and tattoos. This style later became known as skinhead style because many of the young men also shaved their heads. At the beginning of the twenty-first century the skinhead lifestyle is less visible but still exists.

After the skinheads, punk style was the next big youth culture that gained momentum in London. The punk movement became visible in the media in the 1980s, but had begun in the mid-1970s in conscious opposition to the hippies (many hippies at that time were in their late twenties or early thirties). The punks took over Doc Martens boots from the skinheads; they tore up their clothing, used safety pins as adornment, and dressed in black, using leather, rubber, and metal. They were fond of Mohawk hairstyles and dyed their hair bright colors.

In the early 1980s, the style among young people again changed radically. An elegant and nostalgic style of dressing became very popular in England—the antithesis of punk style. The people adopting this style were called Sloane Rangers because they gathered in the area around Sloane Square in London. Before she became Princess of Wales, Lady Diana Spencer was the quintessence of a Sloane Ranger. This was the British equivalent of the yuppie style.

London is one of Europe's largest cities and—like other big European metropolises—is also a major arts center. Many people in the theater, movie, and television business live in London. At one time in the 1990s, more than 10,000 painters and sculptors—a quarter of the total number of artists in Great Britain—lived in East London alone. In Europe, Great Britain is known for having low taxes, which has attracted a huge number of wealthy and industrious people from other countries. Also, for centuries the style-conscious aristocracy has often had residences not only in the countryside, but also in London proper. In addition, like big cities all over the Western world, London has an overrepresentation of gay men. A lot of different types of people visit London, but the appeal to people who like to enjoy the arts is especially strong.

MILAN

Milan is the most important city in northern Italy and the center of one of the most innovative cultures producing durable consumer goods. Northern Italy has a long tradition of skilled craftsmen, and, in combination with the Italian aesthetic, this tradition has given Milan a very decisive influence on design worldwide. In the mountain villages of northern Italy, you will rarely hear a craftsman or a small manufacturer say: "That can't be done." They say: "Let's try." Italians have been successful in all the product categories that we now associate with lifestyle design, from fashion and furniture to cars and food. Northern Italy is also the center of Europe's eyewear industry.

Milan became part of the world's "fashion axis" (along with Paris, New York, and London) in the 1980s. At that time, businessman Leslie Wexner had been very successful in bringing European fashion trends to the United States through The Limited, a chain of fashion stores. In 1982, he decided to take European trends in lingerie to the United States. Years later, he commented on his inspiration in buying the Victoria's Secret chain of lingerie stores: "Like most people, all [the market analysts] could see was that American women shopped for underwear in department stores—and, therefore, they always would. That was not my experience. I had seen women in Paris, London, . . . and Milan buying lingerie in marvelous little boutiques. They saw it as fashion. I was convinced that American women would, too." They certainly would. Today there are more than 1,000 Victoria's Secret stores in the United States and a very successful mail-order catalogue. American women are now buying lingerie in the style of European fashion lingerie, not only at Victoria's Secret stores, but also at La Perla, Italy's number one lingerie brand and Europe's market leader in fashionable lingerie. La Perla also has stores all over the world.

Milan is home to many of Italy's industrial and furniture designers and may very well have the largest number of creative people per capita of any big city in the world. According to an article in the *Harvard Business Review*, there is "a free-floating community of architects, suppliers, photographers, critics, curators, publishers, and craftsmen, among many other categories of professionals, as well as the expected artists and designers." Since the 1980s, Milan has been one of the most popular destinations for young European designers in search of training and work.

Milan is the home base of Giorgio Armani, Versace, Dolce & Gabbana, and many other famous Italian fashion designers. Unlike the other cities mentioned in this chapter, Milan has not spawned an underground youth culture that has expanded beyond the city and become global. But Italians of all ages—not least the Milanese—have been extremely style-conscious for several decades and have routinely proved it by spending a lot of money on commercial fashion products. To many Italians, the principal Milanese designers are household names. Italy has more designer stores than any other country, and Italians buy more designer brands than consumers in any other country. Even Italian children are often dressed in designer clothing.

The designer influence is visible in many parts of the city, but it is along the Via Montenapoleone and the surrounding streets that most of the top designers have their stores. There is perhaps no other shopping street in the world where so many top designer stores can be found in such close proximity.

Rome is Italy's largest city, but Milan, in addition to being its fashion and design center, is also the nation's financial center, which connects many wealthy people to the city.

TOKYO

So far in our story, there have been only a couple of references to Tokyo, but let's leave no stone unturned and have a closer look at Tokyo's influence on Western style and taste.

In Europe and in the United States, copying was widespread in the fashion industry after World War II. In Japan, the focus was more on copying everything, from Leica cameras to Adidas sports shoes. That was what Phil Knight realized when he traveled to Tokyo in 1962. He saw imitation Adidas running shoes in the stores, and he decided that he wanted to import these high-quality sports shoes to the United States. Importing these Japanese shoes was the reason that a short time later he founded what today is known as Nike Inc. The Japanese business of copying Western products played an important role in making many kinds of products cheaper for Western consumers in the second half of the twentieth century. (Today other countries have taken over this role.)

The Tokyo youth culture started growing in the 1980s, as mentioned in Chapter 2. During that decade, many Western fashion designers went to Tokyo for inspiration; at the same time, a group of Japanese designers made breakthroughs in Europe after showing their collections in Paris. The Japanese designers showcased a new style featuring dramatic clothing. This is what the fashion editor of the *International Herald Tribune*, Suzy Menkes, was commenting on when she wrote that there has been a "dramatic and enduring influence of the Japanese aesthetic on European fashion." This also attracted many Western designers to Tokyo, where they found a vibrant youth culture with teenagers who dress in unique ways.

In the 1990s, style trends from Tokyo continued to spread to other parts of the world. One example is the mixing of clothing in highly individual styles. In the spring of 1999, the Japanese singer and collage artist Kahimi Karie, in an interview with American *Vogue*, described her style as "a grey-and-orange windbreaker evoking 1980s Atari games, a kid-size pair of rare 1970s Levi's that flare at the foot, and a symmetrical haircut that would have made Vidal Sassoon—circa 1964—proud." The journalist asked her how she would describe this innovative style. Her answer: "Very Tokyo." Karie also told the reporter: "People in Tokyo are beyond curious—they're addicted to discovering 'the new,' whether it's something retro they haven't seen before or something very modern." This Tokyo-based style came to play a big part in the retro style that appeared in fashion at the beginning of the twenty-first century.

As in all other major cities, each district in Tokyo has its own character and atmosphere. Ginza is where many luxury designer brands have their stores. Shinjuku is the district for young people who are into trendy fashion. Near the Harajuku train station, the style is dramatic and streety. The center of Harajuku is a street named Takeshita-dori. It is in this area that companies like Sony and other electronics companies test new products. If at least 15 percent of the teenagers in Harajuku adopt a new product, the companies are confident that the product will be a success, and they introduce it to other markets. As a journalist wrote in an article about Tokyo: "Takeshita Dori is a little over 300 meters long, but it's so jammed with teenagers, traders, market researchers and fashion journalists that it takes a good 20 minutes to get though to the other end." If we go back to 1993, it was in this area that a teenage boy named Nigo started selling homemade T-shirts with printed images from the science fiction movie *Planet of the Apes*. He ended up founding the company A Bathing Ape and making quirky T-shirt prints a worldwide phenomenon.

In 2007 the *Wall Street Journal* reported that A Bathing Ape helped push men's all-over-print hooded jackets "into the U.S. from Tokyo a couple of seasons ago, prompting small retailers like Union in New York's Soho neighborhood, Barneys Co-op and Internet stores . . . to start selling their own versions. Soon, print hoodies were showing up in hip magazines . . . and hip-hop videos. Over the past six months, more mainstream designers and apparel makers picked up the style, which is now widely available."

As the trade relationship between Japan and the West has grown, the Japanese have introduced products created in Japan in areas like consumer electronics and other such product categories to the West. This is very notable in cars (especially small cars), motorcycles (sporty motorcycles, as discussed in Chapter 5), portable music players (for instance, the Sony Walkman), interior design (Japan has a very strong minimalist tradition), and food, especially sushi. In Japan, sushi was originally fast food for laborers.

Novelist Jay McInerney (who is also an avid food and wine connoisseur) has written: "When I first tried sushi in Tokyo in the autumn of 1977, I thought of myself as an intrepid culinary adventurer, who, if he survived the experience, would return to America to tell the incredible, unbelievable tale of the day he ate raw fish on rice balls. Someday, perhaps, I would tell my children. By the time I returned to the States two years later, I found sushi bars in Midtown Manhattan; within a few years, nigiri sushi had become the signature forage of the Young Urban Professional."

It was in the 1970s that "an increasing number of people in New York, Los Angeles, San Francisco, and Chicago became increasingly familiar with the increasing number of sushi restaurants in their cities" to quote *Vanity Fair*. As the magazine also reported, sushi became mainstream in the United States when a place called Tiger Sushi opened at the Mall of America in Minnesota in 2004. In Paris sushi became a big hit with the fashion crowd by way of the Japanese fashion designers who moved to that city in the 1970s. In London, sushi has become more popular as a lunchtime snack than the classic egg and cress sandwich. And sushi in the shape of California rolls has become a part of what is known as California cuisine.

As the world's largest metropolitan area, with about 35 million people (a third of Japan's population lives in the Greater Tokyo area), Tokyo has all the qualities needed to attract many polysocial groups.

THE TRENDY DISTRICTS

A present-day big city is not one cohesive unit and certainly not one community. In reality, many of the world's largest cities are an amalgamation of "villages." All big cities are very different from district to district, in some cases because of social and cultural/ethnic differences.

Trend creators and trendsetters often go to the world's big cities for inspiration (or they may live in one or more of them). Sometimes they are aware of the historical status of these cities as suppliers of new trends, and are also aware that there are certain districts in which they have a better chance of spotting new trends.

Since the late 1800s, there have been districts in many European and American cities that have had a particular appeal to trendsetters. Many of the districts have a history of being areas where artists lived. In New York, Greenwich Village is the most famous such district. In Paris, Montmartre was the district in which many artists settled. In Milan, the area around Via Brera was considered a Milanese Montmartre. In London, Soho was the bohemian district for many years, attracting "negro actors, lawyers, engineers, dockers up from Wales, waiters, dancers, students, merchant seamen, laborers and musicians," as a 1946 guidebook to London put it.

In fact, many big cities had bohemian districts that have since attracted other trendsetting groups. Greenwich Village became a gay mecca in the 1950s because, as Edmund White writes in his autobiography, "the only milieu where we were welcome as gay men was the bohemian . . . the straight actors, dancers, painters and writers."

The reasons for these districts' appeal might be cheap housing or the availability of artists' studios. The exact districts where the trendsetters meet change from time to time. In the case of Montmartre, this district first became a gathering place for artists because it was outside the official Paris city limits. Wine, therefore, could be sold at a lower price than inside the city limits. When tourists began to flock to Montmartre, the artists moved to the opposite side of Paris: Montparnasse. Later, when the tourists started showing up there, the next district with appeal to artists and the emerging youth culture was the Latin Quarter.

At the end of the 1990s, trendsetters went to Soho in New York, Notting Hill in London, and the Marais in Paris. When word had spread that these areas were trendy, they became uninteresting to the trendsetters, who moved on to new territories. Within these territories, there are likely to be many meeting places for trendsetters: stores, restaurants, hotels, bars, clubs, and other such venues. But they too change from time to time.

At the beginning of the twenty-first century, trendsetter territories in many big cities had once again moved. In the 1980s, thousands of London artists began moving to the East End—to areas such as Hoxton, Clerkenwell, and Shoreditch. Designers, tailors, furniture makers, and traditional craftsmen also moved to the East End, and galleries, stores, and clubs followed. In Paris, rue Oberkampf became the hot new meeting place. In New York, it was the Meatpacking District.

In Los Angeles, artists have lived on the city's West Side for many years. In 1989, the artist Mike Kelley—who became one of the world's most influential artists in the 1990s—moved to the city's East Side. Twelve years later, the American magazine *W* reported about Los Angeles: "Fueled by the recent explosion of gallery activity in Chinatown and the sudden influx of artists nesting in the neighborhoods like Eagle Rock, Highland Park, and Mount Washington, the East Side is blossoming into a virtual hive of creative and commercial activity. Studios, cutting-edge boutiques, bars and cafés are popping up at warp speed, and weekends along Chung King Road are luring an eclectic crowd of hip celebs, intrepid fashionistas and art students from nearby California Art Institute and Art Center."

FROM LOCAL TO GLOBAL

Historically, at least since the Renaissance, there have been entire cities that have had a strong economic and cultural influence on the rest of the world. For many centuries, the world's power center was in Europe. But in the middle of the 1800s, it shifted to the United States. According to the French political scientist Jacques Attali, the world's economic and cultural power centers have been in the following locations since the beginning of the 1300s:

Year	Cultural Center
1300–1450	Bruges
1450–1500	Venice
1500–1550	Antwerp
1550–1650	Genoa
1650–1750	Amsterdam
1750–1850	London
1850–1930	Boston
1930–1980	New York City
1980–2000	Los Angeles/San Francisco

Each of these cities had an enormous influence on the rest of the world's cultural and economic development at the time.

This was not just because of their military or political power, but because of the ideas and innovations that they produced. The city or region that produces the most original and powerful new ideas becomes the cultural center that influences the rest of the world, according to Attali.

The nine cities identified by Attali as historically dominant cultural centers are all either on the sea or have easy access to the sea, making many international shipping connections possible. For centuries, it was through shipping connections that trends spread internationally. This is evident, for instance, in the spread of tattooing.

Tattoos were originally a local custom in Polynesia (including Tahiti), in the Pacific Ocean. European explorers started traveling to Polynesia in the late 1500s, but almost two centuries passed before we find documented evidence of Europeans getting tattoos there. In the second half of the 1700s, when London was the world's cultural center, English explorers, merchants, and sailors began exploring the Pacific. Some of the best-known explorers of the time were Captain James Cook and Captain Samuel Wallis. In 1767, Wallis noticed that getting their bodies painted with thin black lines representing different figures was a universal custom among Tahitian men and women. In 1774, Cook, returning from his trip to the Marquesas Islands, wrote in his diary that "they print signs on people's body and call this tattow." A Tahitian man named Ma'i (called Omai by the English), the first Tahitian to travel to Europe (with Cook), became famous partly because of his tattoos.

Sailors going to Polynesia began getting tattoos as souvenirs, and tattoos became part of the merchant marine and navy culture. In the following centuries, tattooing spread to other countries as more and more sailors—who were then the world's globetrotters—visited Polynesia and got their own tattoos. As tattoo parlors became common in port cities, nonsailors began to get tattoos as well.

In the twenty-first century a city's ability to set and spread trends still depends on how widely connected it is to other big cities. However, since the 1960s, "widely connected to other cities" primarily means having the most domestic and international flight connections. Trends from places that are off the beaten flight paths rarely go beyond the city or region in which they start, even though these trends can certainly have a major local or regional impact.

To identify the cities with the greatest chance of influencing style and taste, we must look for the cities with the most connections to other locations. In the 1960s, the busiest long-distance routes on a global scale were those between New York and California and New York–London. New York–Tokyo and San Francisco–Tokyo were also major (and very busy) routes. At the end of the twentieth century, the same routes continued to be the world's most trafficked routes, but London–Tokyo is now also one of the world's busiest international routes.

On a global scale, New York, Los Angeles, London, Paris, San Francisco, Tokyo, and Milan have the most flight connections, both domestically and internationally, and they are widely connected to each other by direct flights. Maps of airline routes out of these seven cities show flights going in almost all directions, with the routes forming a multipointed star-shaped pattern (see Figure 4.1). This pattern mirrors the way in which trends spread between people, as discussed in Chapter 2. And this pattern is important if trends are to get momentum on an international scale.

In the United States, a new trend may start in Los Angeles or New York and then spread in all directions at the same time. It can quickly spread to Chicago, Austin, Miami, Boston, and Atlanta. From these cities, it will again spread in a multipointed star-shaped pattern to smaller cities. On a global level, trends also spread in multipointed star-shaped patterns. For instance, a trend

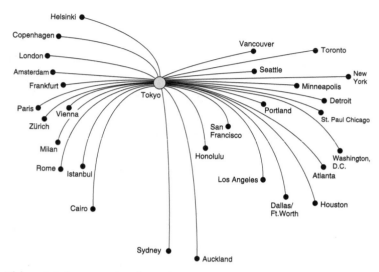

Figure 4.1 An example of a multipointed star-shaped airline route map (of intercontinental flights out of Tokyo)

can spread from Los Angeles to London, Paris, and, in principle, many other European cities simultaneously.

There is no indication that trendsetters travel more than other people. The only difference between trendsetters and other travelers is that trendsetters are keen observers of the trendsetting environments found in the world's major cities. When they travel trendsetters are more apt to go to cities and neighborhoods where they can observe trend creators and other trendsetters. When cities with many trendsetters also attract a lot of trendsetters as visitors, it becomes more likely that trends from these cities will spread nationally and/or globally.

By looking at three shoe trends that emerged at the end of the twentieth century in three different places, the importance of these large cities becomes clear. We can start with one shoe case that is already famous: in his best-selling book *The Tipping Point*, journalist Malcolm Gladwell described the sudden rise in sales figures for Hush Puppies shoes in the early 1990s—though he did not explain why and how it happened (more on the explanation issue in Chapter 6). In fact, it was part of a typical trend process.

VIA NEW YORK

Hush Puppies have been produced by a division of Wolverine World Wide, a leading maker of casual, work, and outdoor footwear, since 1958. The brand came into existence when the first sales manager of Wolverine World Wide, Jim Muir, needed a name for a model of comfortable slip-on suede shoes with a lightweight sole. He decided to call them Hush Puppies, and the shoe brand got a tired-looking basset hound as a mascot and logo. A loafer version of Hush Puppies was called Earls, and a lace-up version was given the name Dukes. All were available in a range of colors.

By the early 1990s, the world had lost interest in Hush Puppies. Annual sales had dropped to 30,000 pairs in 1994. The shoes were sold mostly to U.S. prisons and in New York's Chinatown. Wolverine's management was ready to stop producing Hush Puppies. The brand was saved because at just about this time, trendsetting youngsters in New York's East Village district developed an interest in vintage clothing, including secondhand Hush Puppies. Jeffrey Miller, a stylist who was working on a commercial for Wolverine World Wide, spotted this new trend. According to *Vogue*, he told the company's management that Hush Puppies were becoming popular again. The company had just decided on a strategy of distancing itself from the old-fashioned Hush Puppies (the "prison models") and wanted to focus on completely new models. Miller suggested that the company should keep the 1950s models—the styles the trendsetters were buying in secondhand stores.

In August and September 1995 a documentary about Isaac Mizrahi and the creation of his autumn 1994 collection (which was shown to the fashion press on April 12, 1994) was shown on American television. *Unzipped* had originally premiered the Sundance Film Festival in January 1995, and it became an instant hit not only with reviewers but also with many gay men because Mizrahi is openly gay in the movie. At the time Mizrahi was wearing the shoes himself, and in the documentary he twice comments on using Hush Puppies shoes and boots in his upcoming catwalk show.

As soon as stylist Jeffrey Miller had spotted trendsetters buying secondhand Hush Puppies, he contacted his friend John Bartlett, then an up-and-coming designer, and asked if he wanted to use Hush Puppies in his menswear collection for autumn 1995. The answer was yes, and Miller found some old Hush Puppies brochures from the 1960s that Bartlett (who is gay) ended up using in the invitations for the show. Fashion journalists and other attendees reported that Bartlett, a trendy designer, was using Hush Puppies in his semiannual fashion show. Miller also contacted other trend-oriented designers and persuaded them to use Hush Puppies in their catwalk shows.

Celebrities like David Bowie and Susan Sarandon were also spotted wearing Hush Puppies shoes. Jeffrey Miller also made sure that an article about the contents of comedian and actress Ellen DeGeneres's closet mentioned that it contained a pair of Hush Puppies.

In Los Angeles, the designer and fashion store owner Joel Fitzgerald put an eight-meter-tall inflatable basset hound—the Hush Puppies mascot and logo—on the roof of his Hollywood store. At the same time, the store next to his was turned into a Hush Puppies store. One of its first customers was the actor Paul Reubens, better known as Pee-wee Herman.

At about this time, Wolverine started designing new versions of the classic Hush Puppies shoes in colors like Day-Glo orange, red, green, and purple and using new materials. In 1995, Wolverine sold 430,000 pairs of the classic Hush Puppies. The sales figure for the year before had been 30,000 pairs. High-end retailers like Saks, Bergdorf Goodman, and Barneys wanted to sell the brand, according to the *Harvard Business Review*. In 1996, Hush Puppies was awarded an Accessory of the Year award by the Council of Fashion Designers of America. That year, 1,720,000 pairs of Hush Puppies shoes were sold. The following year, the sales figures were even higher.

At the end of the 1990s, Hush Puppies were often featured in international lifestyle magazines—in the October 1997 issue of the gay magazine *Attitude*, for example, and a month later in the trendy women's magazine *Jane*. Wolverine continued to introduce new Hush Puppies lines, including lounge slippers in fancy color combinations and bathing slippers in white terry cloth.

The trend that had started in the East Village had not only revitalized the brand in the United States, but also made the Hush Puppies brand an international success. More than a decade after the trend started, "Hush Puppies are now available in 80 countries around the globe," according to the Hush Puppies Web site. In a small country like Denmark, the number one department store was selling Hush Puppies shoes a decade after the management of the company had almost decided to stop selling the brand.

The interest in Hush Puppies shoes was not just about kitschy shoes; it was about a general interest in thrift-shop clothing, a trend that, for instance, was noted in a 1998 book about consumer behavior. And retro styles were then being presented at fashion shows in major cities, as mentioned in Chapter 1. So, in fact, the interest in Hush Puppies shoes in the early 1990s was an early sign of the retro trend that would explode around 2000. In the late 1990s, there was the interest in "boho" style, as mentioned in Chapter 2, and there were many other clues, not least the interest in vintage clothing among Hollywood celebrities.

In furniture, there was a renewed interest in Scandinavian furniture from the 1950s, and in cars, several retro models were introduced (more on this in Chapter 7). In music, hits from the 1970s and 1980s were being remade. Hush Puppies themselves were a fad, but the fad that lasted long enough and got enough attention to get others hooked. And 10 years later, there was the revival of the Jackie Kennedy style for a couple of seasons. This was yet another variation on the retro trend that kept the trendsetters' interest boiling, showing us that fads can sometimes be an ingredient in a trend. However, generally fads are just that—fads.

VIA MILAN

Birkenstock is the name of a German family of shoemakers. The family began making shoes in Langenberg, Germany, in 1774. In 1897, a Birkenstock shoemaker got the idea of making a lightweight sole out of cork. It later turned out that this sole could be used for foot-shaped sandals—for which Birkenstock became famous in the 1960s.

In the 1960s, many hippies and other people who were into alternative health started wearing the foot-shaped Birkenstock sandals. The sandals became especially popular among liberals. In fact, wearing Birkenstock sandals became more or less synonymous with being politically liberal, so much so that they were a tough sell outside of these circles. This was what Margot Fraser experienced in 1966 when she began importing Birkenstock sandals to the United States. The sandals' appeal was limited strictly to the hippie and alternative health markets. On the positive side, these customers were extremely loyal to Birkenstock. In the 1980s the sandals were not trendy. By the late 1990s, however, Birkenstock sandals had become the coolest pair of shoes you could slip your feet into, thanks to a young American fashion designer named Narciso Rodriguez. In 1995, Rodriguez had

been appointed design director at the French fashion label
Cerutti in Paris. In 1996 he designed the dress his friend Carolyn
Bessette wore when she married John F. Kennedy, Jr. The following year, Rodriguez was appointed design director of the
Spanish luxury leather house Loewe, owned by the fashion con-
glomerate LVMH (which also owns Louis Vuitton). In October
1997, he showed his first women's ready-to-wear collection
under the Narciso Rodriguez label. In February 1998, Rodriguez
was given the best new designer award by the Council of Fashion
Designers of America.

In March 1998, Rodriguez showed his second collection in
Milan; the models were wearing light chiffon dresses and the
most traditional of the Birkenstock foot-shaped sandals. The
international fashion press was present, as were purchasers from
both Europe and the United States, and there were many stylists
and makeup artists both backstage and in the audience.

Designers in other countries copied the Birkenstock trend in their
own shows the following season. At one such show in Copenhagen,
Denmark, in August 1998, I remember sitting next to a fashion journalist who said: "I think now is the time to invest in Birkenstock
shares!" Many of the models were wearing Birkenstock sandals. It
created quite a buzz. After that, Birkenstock sandals were featured in
the trendsetting fashion magazines, and the trendsetters quickly
adopted the old "alternative health" sandal. Both men and women
in the fashion industry started wearing Birkenstocks. Suddenly
young women who would not have been caught dead wearing the
sandals just a few seasons earlier were buying them in droves.

In a 1999 article in the magazine *Miami Metro*, a man said: "I
combine them with socks—it's a German thing." In 2002 the
trendy men's magazine *Arena* championed Birkenstock's Arizona
sandal as one of the most popular sandals for men. In 2003, there
were "queues around the block at the Birkenstock store in
Covent Garden [in central London] for its one-strap Madrid

sandals [that] were being worn by everyone from *Vogue* editors to supermodels," according to the *Guardian*.

Birkenstock has launched a product development and design program that included Birkenstock sandals as reinterpreted and reinvented by supermodel Heidi Klum. In 2005, Birkenstock sandals were featured in many magazines, for instance, *Self*, *Lucky*, *Elle*, *Fit Pregnancy*, *Playboy*, *Cargo*, *Out*, *Runner's World*, and *Country Living*, most of which have broad mainstream appeal.

There certainly was also a distinct retro touch to the interest in Birkenstock shoes, showing that the retro trend was going from simmering to boiling.

VIA LOS ANGELES

Ugg boots is both a generic term for Australian flat-heeled, pull-on sheepskin boots and a brand name in the United States and other countries. They were originally created by shearers, who wrapped Merino sheepskins around their feet to keep them warm. Other Australians also started wearing the boots. The name is derived from the word *ugly*, and these "ugly boots" have been made in Australia for most of the twentieth century. The sheepskin boots were mostly used indoors, but some people also wore them when they went outdoors and even when going grocery shopping. They were considered mostly "working class" in Australia until the beginning of the twenty-first century, when they became an international trend.

The sheepskin boots are comfortable to wear year-round. In cold weather, they keep the feet warm, and in warm weather, the natural fibers of the fleece have a cooling effect on the feet by wicking away perspiration. In the 1970s, Australian surfers began using them to warm up their feet after surfing in cold water for hours. The surfers also found that their sheepskin boots were comfortable in winter after skiing.

American surfers who had been to Australia also started wearing the boots during the 1970s. At that time, you could buy Ugg boots only in Australia. In 1978 an Australian surfer named Brian Smith went to the United States with a few pairs of Ugg boots in his rucksack. He tried to sell them in New York, with no success, but when he went to Los Angeles, he found his market. He set up a company and started selling Ugg boots in the United States.

In the early 1990s, when surfing became more and more popular as both a professional and a recreational sport, the market for sheepskin boots grew. At the time, the television show *Baywatch* was one of the most popular U.S. TV series. One of the original members of the cast was actress Pamela Anderson, who was also one of the first celebrities to be seen wearing the sheepskin boots, both on and off the show. In the beginning of the 2000s, Ugg boots had become popular with college women all over the United States. Many of them bought the boots through the Internet.

Another trendsetter who took up Uggs was Lucy Benzecry, the owner of a boutique named West Village in London. She had been wearing and selling them at her store for years before they became popular. When the gossip magazines started writing about the many celebrities who were wearing them, the store was besieged by shoppers wanting the boots.

That year the *Guardian* newspaper listed all the celebrities who had been photographed wearing them: Madonna, Gwyneth Paltrow, Sarah Jessica Parker, Kate Hudson, Cameron Diaz, Nicole Kidman, Leonardo DiCaprio, Reese Witherspoon, Jennifer Aniston, Jennifer Lopez, and Julia Roberts. In 2003, the U.S. department store chain Nordstrom staged a traveling exhibition of a collection of Ugg boots with decoration by celebrities Lucy Liu, Britney Spears, and Anjelica Huston. They were later auctioned off for charity.

The new popularity of the boots sparked new product development. Different manufacturers started producing sheepskin boots in pink, lavender, baby blue, and other colors. Some were even embroidered or trimmed with lace. Several of the big manufacturers had to outsource to China to keep up with the demand. Some even started to produce the boots out of synthetic materials, making the boots affordable to more people.

One clear pattern is that again and again, the trends that have had the biggest influence not just in single countries but in most of the world have come from the same places—actually just a little more than a handful of major cities that share some important characteristics, the most important being that they are home to many polysocial groups and that they appeal to visitors who belong to polysocial groups. The original product, design, or style does not have to be created in one of these cities—in fact, it can come from almost anywhere.

TREND-SPOTTING CLUES

When we want to spot new and emerging trends, we can learn from the trend characteristics covered in this chapter:

- There are only a limited number of cities that have the characteristics that will make a trend spread nationally or globally.
- The more connected a trendsetting city is to the rest of the world, the greater the chance that trends from the city will go global.
- The greater the variety of trendsetters in a city, the more trendsetting that city will be.
- The following cities have a history of being places where many global trends have started: Los Angeles, San Francisco, New York, London, Paris, Milan, and Tokyo.

- The more a certain type of trend emerges from a particular city, the greater the likelihood that similar trends will emerge from this city.
- The trendsetters cluster in certain districts within the world's big cities, often districts that have a history of being home to polysocial groups.

5

THE PLOT THICKENS

THICKENS

DISSECTING REAL-LIFE
TRENDS

We know now that the start of a trend is a unique and complex social process that in fact does not happen very often. But when it does happen, several factors are at work:

- Only when several groups that are polysocial embrace a new trend will it get enough momentum to spread.
- Only when a large number of trendsetters in each of the polysocial groups embrace the trend will it get the attention of the trend followers.
- Media that appeal to polysocial groups must report on the trend for the trend to get momentum.

This is exactly what happened with disco music. In 1976, "disco music was heard only by small urban groups of blacks and Hispanics, homosexuals and Beautiful Insomniacs who turned dozens of off-the-beaten-path discotèques into after-hours shrines," *Newsweek* wrote in a cover story in 1979. The cover story headline was "Disco Takes Over." According to the magazine, "Nobody has been more surprised by the disco take-over than the major record-company executives. Until recently, they viewed the disco beat as a passing fancy." Well, they had not recognized the influence of polysocial groups.

The pattern highlighted in Figure 2.2 is very important early in the trend process because there have to be enough trendsetters for the new style or sound to be observed. If, for instance, artists, celebrities, and gay men adopt a style, it is more likely that it will become a trend than if only artists adopt the style. We saw this also in Chapter 1 with minimalism, which was adopted by multiple groups, including designers, wealthy people, and gay men.

So, what does it take for a new style to attract the interest of enough trendsetters to become a trend? The best way to answer this question is to document and analyze different trends that have evolved through the entire Diamond-Shaped Trend Model, paying extra attention to the early phases of the trend process. By dissecting four historical trends, we can determine whether there are patterns of what attracts the trendsetters in the early evolution of a trend. The four cases are these:

- Blue jeans
- Motorcycles
- Inline skates
- Apple's iPod

BLUE JEANS

The origin of blue jeans goes back to the middle of the 1800s, to California, for it was in 1853 that a German-born immigrant named Levi Strauss settled in San Francisco and created one of the most enduring and popular clothing designs that the world has ever seen.

Levi Strauss was 24 years old when he arrived in San Francisco after having lived in New York City for four years. He planned to make a living by selling dry goods to the people prospecting for gold to the north of the city. He started by selling his entire stock of fabric to fellow passengers on the five-month journey by sea from the East Coast to the West Coast. The only fabric he could not sell was some canvas for use in making tents. The young trader, therefore, took the canvas to the gold prospectors in northern California. They, however, did not want fabric for tents;

they wanted trousers—strong, robust trousers were what they needed most. This prompted the young entrepreneur to start manufacturing trousers for them.

The prospectors were very happy with the new canvas trousers, and word of them spread all over northern California. When Strauss ran out of canvas, he started using denim. This did not decrease the demand; on the contrary, it seemed that every prospector in northern California wanted to wear "waist-high overalls," as Strauss called his new trousers. The following year, in 1854, Strauss started using the stitching that creates the double-winged logo on the back pocket.

In 1872, a young tailor by the name of Jacob Davis, who had emigrated from Latvia, contacted Strauss. He had developed a technique for using metal rivets to make trousers more durable. The technique was patented and was incorporated into the Levi Strauss trousers. At the same time, orange stitching was used on the trousers to match the copper rivets. And in 1886 the leather label above the right back pocket was added.

At the end of the Gold Rush, blue jeans could easily have disappeared. But many former prospectors got work as ranch hands, and they kept on wearing their denim trousers when they became cowboys. This made blue jeans part of the cowboy work uniform.

The most famous Levi Strauss blue jeans style, 501, got its number in 1890 and became the core of the product line. Also that year, a new pocket for a watch was introduced. In 1905, the style got an extra back pocket, which became the fifth and last pocket.

San Francisco was an important port city at the time, and many sailors also started wearing denim trousers. It was because of the sailors that blue jeans eventually got that name. Jeans were originally a type of cotton trousers worn by sailors from the northern Italian port city of Genoa. The French called these trousers *genes*, which became *jeans* in the United States (though this did not become the official term for this type of trousers until the mid-1930s, decades after Strauss died in 1902).

Other entrepreneurs also started manufacturing blue jeans. Companies like Wrangler and Lee became major suppliers of blue jeans in the twentieth century. And over time Levi's continued developing its product, adding belt loops in 1922 and a zipper instead of a button fly in 1926. And in 1938 the company started to reach a new market by introducing blue jeans for women.

Levi's blue denim jeans were popular in farming communities all over the West at the beginning of the twentieth century, but blue denim jeans were little known in the East until the 1930s. This changed during the Depression, when many ranch owners had to find new sources of income. Therefore, they started opening up their ranches to people from the East (then often called "dudes") who wanted to enjoy the adventure of a Western ranch vacation. Many vacationers at the dude ranches took their blue jeans back to the big cities on the East Coast. Thus, blue jeans went from being part of rural life to becoming an urban phenomenon, though this process was slowed down by World War II. After World War II, however, blue denim trousers became a full part of the new urban landscape.

When Wrangler was founded in 1947, it targeted ranchers in its product development strategy and was one of the first blue jeans manufacturers to use market research in its development process. As a result, Wrangler became the preferred brand of cowboys and rodeo performers after World War II. Levi's became the preferred brand of the urban phenomenon known as bikers. In many cases, the bikers identified with cowboys as the free spirits of the prairie and adopted part of the cowboys' dress: the blue jeans and the leather chaps. Of course, they replaced the horse with the motorcycle.

The music and film industries also played an important part in popularizing blue jeans in the cities. The singing cowboys of the 1940s, the most famous of whom were Roy Rogers and Bob Wills, had a lot of success during a period of industrialization and urbanization, when many Americans were nostalgic for the "Old West." Their songs romanticized prairie life. The musical genre that Roy Rogers, Bob Wills, and the other singing cowboys created became one of the roots of today's country-and-western music. Though the number of actual ranch workers decreased after World War II, the popularity of country-and-western grew. Blue jeans became the preferred clothing style of many country-and-western performers and their fans.

As for movies, Western movies were one of the most popular film genres after World War II. With movies such as *The Far Country* (1954) and *Rio Bravo* (1959), Hollywood played a major role in making blue jeans popular; they became a symbol of freedom—and, in Europe, also a symbol of America. In Europe, blue jeans were almost unknown before World War II, but as the American military presence in Europe grew at the end of the war and after it, many Europeans became familiar with blue jeans as well as many other American products. For instance, in Sweden, the first pair of blue jeans was sold in 1947.

In movies of the 1950s, such as *The Wild One* with Marlon Brando and *Giant* with James Dean, millions of people could see attractive men wearing blue jeans. In the 1950s and 1960s, product development of blue jeans continued, so that each new generation could have its own style, including black jeans, which were introduced in 1952, and bleached jeans, which were introduced by Lee in 1969.

In the 1960s, the new youth culture, the hippies, also favored blue jeans because of the rebel and working-class image that blue jeans had. One new style was blue jeans that were sewn together in a V at the knee and wider at the ankles. Many models had so much width that they looked like bells, so they were logically named bell-bottoms.

Blue jeans were revolutionizing everyday clothing. In 1966, then 17-year old Meredith Hall was to attend her last year of high school at a new school in New Hampshire. In her memoir she writes about meeting her fellow students and teachers for the first time: "Their clothes are strange. . . . The girls and boys both wear faded Levi's and loose shirts, untucked. They are barefoot in the warm September sun, although class will start soon. In fact, some of the teachers sit in the sun with us, wearing the same faded jeans and loose shirts and talking with the students easily. I have never seen anyone like these people. . . . I am an observer."

In 1968, then 16-year-old Lynn Darling enrolled at Harvard University. She had never worn blue jeans before, and when she started wearing them she did not tell her mother because, as she writes in her memoirs, "blue jeans change everything." It was about this time that punk rock singer Patti Smith in New York initiated the trend for ripped or shredded jeans, which became characteristic of punk style (as mentioned in Chapter 2).

When the hypermasculine look with tattoos and crew-cut hair became popular among gay men in the 1970s (as mentioned in Chapters 2 and 4 respectively), Levi's 501s became part of a new "gay uniform," very much inspired by the biker look. At the end of the 1970s, the fashionable blue jeans were fitted and tight. For some, the preferred style was jeans that were so tight that they looked as though they were glued on. Some girls had to lie down in order to get the jeans on. There were stories in the media about young girls who could not get the jeans off without the help of friends.

Blue jeans also had to look torn and worn. Getting new jeans to look properly worn became almost a science. Parents were appalled when their teenage sons and daughters bought a new pair of jeans and immediately began treating it with sandpaper. To some young men, it was so important that they had the right worn look that they wouldn't take their jeans off for long periods of time, sometimes weeks and even months. A young man named Angelo from New York City became the record holder for wearing his jeans the longest: eight months. Somehow, he managed to keep his family from discovering that not only had he not changed his blue jeans, but he had also actually kept them on when showering and sleeping.

Sales at Levi Strauss & Co. were going up all the time. At one point in the 1980s, the company had sold more than 600 million pairs of blue jeans since its founding. Posthumously, Levi Strauss and Jacob Davis were both awarded the prestigious Coty Special Award for their design.

At the beginning of the 1970s, three companies more or less "owned" the blue jeans category: Levi's, Lee, and Wrangler. But this changed when a large Hong Kong–based clothing manufacturing company by the name of Murjani actively sought a famous designer who would lend his or her name to a new brand of blue jeans. However, as no designer wanted his or her name associated with blue jeans, Murjani started asking "American royalty" such as the Rockefellers and Jacqueline Kennedy Onassis if Murjani could use their names for a big fee. The answer was no until heiress Gloria Vanderbilt accepted a deal. The Vanderbilt jeans went on sale in 1976, and "the jeans exploded like cork out of champagne bottle. . . . Well-dressed women everywhere were wearing jeans, and Vanderbilt's brand became so popular with women that sociologists . . . began pondering the trend," according to the Calvin Klein biography *Obsession*. A couple of years later Gloria Vanderbilt Jeans had the largest share of the market.

When fashion designers such as Giorgio Armani, Calvin Klein, and Ralph Lauren also began manufacturing blue jeans, the term *designer jeans* came into existence. Calvin Klein launched his sexy jeans for women in 1978, and about a year later he had a 20 percent share of the market. When the designer launched blue jeans for men, sales rose by 30 percent.

At the end of the 1980s and the beginning of the 1990s, skaters and hip-hop artists dominated youth culture. Both groups preferred baggy jeans. To the skaters, this was the obvious choice for functional reasons. The hip-hop artists also wore sports clothing, especially nylon pants by Adidas and Nike. These two groups were not interested in wearing—or being associated with—tight Levi's blue jeans.

As Levi's were still preferred by country-and-western fans and other consumers, and as the brand was considered among the strongest in the business, Levi Strauss's management did not invest in significant new product development. But the designer brands did. They were aware that they were in the fashion business—that is, they knew they had to introduce new models each season and create or follow the trends that other brands set. The Italian fashion brand Prada introduced a new minimalist look, with lots of nylon fabrics, that became popular among trendsetters in the middle 1990s making denim look old-fashioned.

Over the years, Levi's jeans came more and more to represent a conservative style. Young people did not want to wear blue jeans. With no exciting new products, Levi's faced a serious crisis in the 1990s; the company had to close down factories and lay off many workers. One of its strategies for dealing with the crisis was to introduce a new brand named Dockers specializing in khaki pants for the mainstream market, in direct competition with the highly successful retail brands Gap and Banana Republic.

When significant new product development was finally introduced in the jeans category in the 1990s, it did not come from the established traditional brands. In 1991, Hidehiko Yamane, who was originally trained as a tailor, established a completely new jeans brand, Evisu, in Japan. He did not like mass-produced jeans, but he loved vintage jeans. In the 1980s, he began importing vintage jeans to Japan. This led him to start creating his own jeans with the vintage look. He bought old American Union Special sewing machines, which had been considered the Rolls-Royce of sewing machines in the 1950s. Using this old-fashioned technology, he was able to produce only 14 pairs of Evisu jeans a day.

The Evisu logo was hand-painted on the jeans. As the Evisu home page states: "Although initially Evisu was more a labor of love than a commercial venture, Evisu jeans captured the imagination of the detail-obsessed Japanese fashion crowd, spurring a revival of interest in vintage denim which has now spread around the world." Evisu jeans started being sold outside of Japan in the second half of the 1990s. Around this time, British soccer player and trendsetter David Beckham was seen wearing Evisu jeans.

In 1995 the stylist Suzanne Costas Freiwald also started manufacturing blue jeans that were different from the mass-produced jeans. She established her blue jeans brand, Earl Jean, in her garage. She had designed a pair of blue jeans for herself because she could not find any she liked in the stores. Her friends immediately wanted to buy the jeans, so she started commercial production. "It was the first slim, low-rise, boot-cut shape, quality jean that ushered in dark denim. It was a whole new paradigm," reported American *Vogue*.

Also in 1995, designer Jerome Dahan of Seven for All Mankind invented "whiskers," or little white lines running across the legs of blue jeans that looked like a wrinkle fade. This started an explosion in wash technology in the garment industry.

At the same time, young trend creators in New York City began decorating their blue jeans with India ink. Also in New York, an artist began offering to paint individual patterns on blue jeans. Fashion designer Helmut Lang began introducing torn jeans, which also had designs with "paint spots." Gucci launched blue jeans with embroidery, pearls, and feathers.

A few years later, Levi Strauss adopted the idea of painting on new pairs of jeans and introduced this concept in a number of its stores. Customers could go into the store and, with or without guidance, paint on their jeans themselves. At the same time, brands manufacturing jeans for the mainstream market began selling jeans with embroidery. Then Gucci introduced its version of torn jeans.

It was only at the end of the 1990s that Levi's began to develop new styles in the jeans category. The company realized that style changes had become important and that you had to not only supply different kinds of blue jeans to different market segments, but also introduce innovative new styles on a regular basis. In the summer of 1999, this resulted in the Levi's Engineered Jeans collection. In the early twenty-first century, Levi's also introduced customized jeans for women.

In 2000, the first reports that there was again demand for blue jeans among young people were heard in the trade. In the spring of 2001, the news at European men's fashion and streetwear fairs was that sales of blue jeans were going up again. In the street and at the trendsetters' meeting places, you could also see that blue jeans had become popular again. In her memoir of being a *New York Post* journalist and relationship columnist Bridget Harrison writes about meeting "a . . . trendy array of people dressed in cargo pants, shredded sweatshirts and ripped jeans" in "a real downtown scene." This was in 2000.

In the spring collections for 2002, Wrangler and other jeans manufacturers introduced authentic-looking jeans styles as well as 1970s vintage looks—boot-cut and worn and torn styles. The styles were clearly influenced by top international designers like Helmut Lang and Marc Jacobs. So much product development was going on that a book called *Jeans + Casuals Insider ABC* was published, giving an overview of all the treatment techniques and styles being used for jeans. The book identified 20 different surface treatments, 20 different weaves and colorings, 8 different standard styles, and more than 40 manufacturers.

In 2000, consumers at the top of the Diamond-Shaped Trend Model were again buying blue jeans, and the market was expanding. At that time, *Vogue* reported that international top designers like Viktor & Rolf, Hussein Chalayan, and Henry Duarte had introduced new denim lines. "Designer denim is on such a manic roll of creativity, it's become the unstoppable fashion phenomenon of our times," the magazine wrote. High-quality Japanese denim and Japanese jeans brands became popular with trendsetters at the beginning of the twenty-first century.

In 2005, *Time Style & Design* reported that the demand for blue jeans with highly sophisticated washes was higher than ever. The ripped jeans style was popular again. In 2006, Levi's introduced its first jeans made with all-natural processes from 100 percent organic cotton—with visible green stitching. It was almost as if blue jeans had been reinvented, and compared to the original Levi's blue jeans, the new blue jeans styles were constantly changing in shape, color, and fabric quality.

Product development certainly seems to play an important role in the position of a style or design in the Diamond-Shaped Trend Model. If we also see this pattern in other categories, we have an important clue that will help us to spot a new trend.

INLINE SKATES

In the 1990s, inline skating became hugely popular. Roller skates had already been popular for many years; in fact, various types of roller skates had even been around since the 1700s. In the 1800s, different people experimented with roller skates; for example, in 1863 an American by the name of James Plimpton made a four-wheel roller skate with two rows of wheels on each skate. However, it was not until after World War II that four-wheel roller skates began to be mass produced, and these models were strapped to regular footwear. In the 1970s, models that combined skate and boot in one unit appeared. The wheels were made of polyurethane and were harder and broader than those on the old models. This made skating a more pleasant experience. Roller skating became a popular leisure activity for many young people. In the 1970s, even roller disco was popular.

The story of the modern inline skate as a fitness gadget began in the United States. In 1980, two hockey-playing brothers, Scott and Brennan Olson, spotted a pair of old inline skates in a sporting goods store in their hometown of Minneapolis, Minnesota. They realized right away that this kind of skate could be a very good dry-land training tool for hockey players. They started redesigning the skates using a hockey boot, polyurethane wheels, and a rubber heel brake. With the new inline skates, they could train in summer in more or less the same way they did in winter on their ice skates. The brothers' inline skates were faster than traditional roller skates, and you did not have to use as much energy to get up to speed on inline skates.

Shortly after they tested their invention, the Olson brothers began selling the new product under the brand name Rollerblade. The first buyers were hockey players, but shortly after the brand was introduced to the market, skiers also began buying the new skates. Demand increased little by little. In 1984, the brothers sold their company, and the new owners had a clear strategy: they wanted to position inline skating as a new sports activity. As part of this strategy, they gave inline skates to the stores in Venice Beach, California, that rented roller skates. Venice Beach had by then become a well-known meeting place for artists, bohemians, muscle fitness enthusiasts, beach bums, and other polysocial groups.

In the late 1980s, Rollerblade launched Team Rollerblade, a group of professional inline skaters who could skate down staircases and stairway banisters in their Rollerblades. Team Rollerblade traveled all over the United States, and also internationally.

One of the team members was the inline skating world champion-to-be, Chris Edwards.

The strategy for launching inline skating as a new sports activity paid off. In the beginning of the 1990s, inline skating was one of the fastest-growing leisure activities in the United States. For a while Rollerblade was the only brand on the market. Competitors like UltraWheels then came into the market, but it was Rollerblade that gave the new sport its unofficial name, rollerblading. The Europeans lagged behind the U.S. market, but inline skating became immensely popular on both continents. In the United States, the number of new entry-level inline skaters increased by almost 50 percent for a number of years, going from 2.5 million in 1989 to 18.5 million in 1995, according to data from American Sports Data.

As the sport grew in popularity, there was a torrent of new product developments in inline skates, including the following:

- K2 introduced Softboot technology (boots made of leather and mesh that the feet can breathe through).
- Nautilus (the manufacturer of gym equipment) developed a Nautilus Skate Machine.
- K2 introduced inline skates developed especially for women.
- UltraWheels introduced an ergonomic inline skate (looking like a snowboard boot with wheels underneath).
- Mission introduced inline skates especially for roller hockey.
- Mojo introduced a skate made of see-through plastic that attached to regular sport shoes (so that you can run when you cannot use the wheels).

Also in this period there were many new events created for inline skaters:

- Roller hockey introduced professional championships that were covered by television.

- The inline skaters began skating on skateboard ramps.
- Inline skate–run events covering distances between 5 and 75 miles emerged.
- Night inline skating became popular—the skaters would wear a helmet with a front light and hold a flashlight.
- Roller basketball was invented by former NBA player Tom LaGarde.

In the media of the period, you could also read the following news stories:

- In 1993, more than 50,000 people contacted the National In-Line Hockey Association to get more information about the sport.
- The New York Road Skaters Association opened a free "emergency room" in Central Park for injured skaters. Volunteers wearing red T-shirts helped injured skaters and gave advice to beginners.
- Scientists from the University of Massachusetts published a study showing that a jogger could burn 14.9 calories per minute, and an inline skater could burn almost as much—14.1 calories. Stepping—another popular fitness activity at the time—burned only 10.8 calories per minute.
- The first annual Extreme Games, broadcast by ESPN, opened on June 24, 1995, and included inline skating.
- In 1997, the magazine *ESPN Total Sports* reported that Arlo Eisenberg was "the Picasso of skating." The 22-year-old was an acrobatic master on his inline skates.

In the 1990s, inline skating became a fitness and leisure trend. At the beginning of the decade, it was a trendsetting fitness activity; by the end of the decade, it was mainstream. But its popularity soon plummeted. Several brands, including Nike, quit making skates, and others cut back. Not as many new product features were introduced to the market as had been previously.

According to the Sporting Goods Manufacturers Association of the United States, the number of inline skaters in the United States who skated at least once a year dropped by almost 50 percent during the seven years between 1998 (at 32 million skaters) and 2004 (down to 17 million skaters).

The same pattern was observed in Europe, according to Sports Tracking Europe. In Europe, sales topped out in the late 1990s. The lack of new, innovative designs and events made the trend-setters and eventually the mainstream consumers lose interest. Once again product development and other innovations played an important role in the popularity of inline skating, and when the innovations slowed down, inline skating was heading toward the bottom half of the Diamond-Shaped Trend Model.

MOTORCYCLES

Until 1903, motorcycles were like regular bicycles with a motor added. But in 1903 the world's first "real" motorcycle was introduced by Harley-Davidson. The motorcycle was given the name Silent Grey Fellow to underline its reliability and dependability. The yield was a modest 3 mph.

In the product development process, the men behind the Harley-Davidson motorcycle—three brothers with the last name Davidson and their friend William S. Harley—had also experimented with putting small engines on bicycles. But the result was never satisfactory because a regular bicycle was too slight to handle a high speed of, say, 25 mph. Arthur Davidson and William Harley decided to build a stronger frame with reinforced rims and ball bearings.

After the success of the first model, another Harley-Davidson model with the characteristic V-twin 45 O-engine was introduced in 1909. This model had two cylinders that were placed at a 45-degree angle so that they formed a V shape. The V shape gave the Harley-Davidson engines the distinct look and sound that they still have today.

During both world wars, Harley-Davidson supplied the U.S. Army. The company also sold motorcycles to police departments around the country and to the national postal service. After World War I, Harley-Davidson was the world's largest motorcycle manufacturer. In 1936 it introduced the so-called knuckle-head engine, the first in a long series of engine product developments. When the company developed a new engine, it was introduced on all models. In the 1950s, the Harley's gasoline tank could hold enough gas to go about 60 miles. Fifty years later it could go more than twice as far.

During World War II, the U.S. Army bought almost 90,000 Harley-Davidson motorcycles. As a result, hundred of thousands of soldiers got to know Harley-Davidson products during their time in the service. In civilian life, after their tour in the army, some of the discharged soldiers wanted their own motorcycles. A number of those soldiers became part of the first Hells Angels club, which was established in 1948 in San Bernardino, California (as detailed in Chapter 4). For many years there were more motorcycles registered in California than in the other 49 states combined. To some, motorcycles became part of an attractive California lifestyle.

In the following decades, the Hells Angels and Harley-Davidson were closely connected because most Hells Angels bikers chose to ride Harley-Davidsons, the number one brand in motorcycles. The Hells Angels bikers were famous for *chopping* their Harleys—that is, stripping the bikes of all unnecessary equipment. This made the bikes look rawer and tougher. Some of them took their motorcycles apart and rebuilt them from the ground up to suit their own personalities and driving styles. In some cases they made the front forks longer and created the kind of motorcycle that today is known as a chopper. In the 1960s,

Harley owners began to give their motorcycles more personalized looks. This started with decorating them with a few knickknacks and/or painting them in different colors and motifs.

In a way, the Hells Angels Motorcycle Club became the unofficial product development department of Harley-Davidson. Many of the personalization and customization ideas that these hard-core bikers came up with were eventually incorporated into Harley-Davidson motorcycles. Hells Angel biker Ralph "Sonny" Barger writes in his autobiography: "The Hells Angels are responsible for a lot of the current designs and workmanship on modern motorcycles. When you look at current custom Softrail motorcycles . . . you see a lot of our design innovations. Our chopper motorcycles inspired even kids' bicycles, like the Schwinn Sting Ray with its banana seat and gooseneck handlebars. . . . Custom motorcycles and bike-riding gear has become a bigger business than ever. Thank the Hells Angels for that."

Hollywood was quick to include the motorcycle lifestyle in the movies. In the 1950s and 1960s, a number of movies that featured Harleys were produced. The one that is best known today is *The Wild One* (1953), with Marlon Brando and Lee Marvin. The movie was based on a true story about the first motorcycle gangs in California. In 1967, the movie *Hells Angels on Wheels* was released. This was Jack Nicholson's first major movie. In 1969, *Easy Rider* was released, featuring Peter Fonda and Dennis Hopper as two rebels who ride a couple of chopped, shining chrome Harleys. In one of the scenes in the movie, they are driving down a seemingly endless highway to the song "Born to Be Wild."

Off the big screen, celebrities such as actor Mickey Rourke, musician Jerry Garcia, and singer Willie Nelson have at one time or another expressed their love for Harleys. In 1991, actor Don Johnson starred in the movie *Harley-Davidson and the Marlboro Man* together with Rourke. All the movies featuring

Harley-Davidson motorcycles have become an important part of the Harley-Davidson myth and brand. Motorcycles came to represent freedom and individualism, two concepts that for many years were seen as representative of the American lifestyle.

Hells Angels motorcycle clubs now exist in many different countries and for many years have had a rebellious image. They have also had a reputation for being connected to crime. In the 1950s, the American Motorcyclist Association wanted to distance itself from the rebel image that motorcyclists were getting in the general population. The association made it clear that 99 percent of the motorcyclists in the United States were law-abiding citizens, and only 1 percent were criminal and antisocial. (Hells Angels bikers turned this statement into something positive for them by saying that they belonged to "the 1 percent," the chosen rebels.)

In the 1950s a new version of the Harley-Davidson motorcycle was introduced—the now classic Electra Glide, which has a big front windshield and a very big and very comfortable seat. This turned out to be the only major product development by Harley-Davidson for a long time. While other factories continued to develop new products, such as police motorcycles and race motorbikes, product development at Harley-Davidson was standing still.

As the economy expanded, more and more people were able to buy motorcycles, especially from the 1960s onward. A number of Japanese manufacturers were highly successful in introducing smaller and more sporty models. Several of these models were far better for driving fast on highways because the driver had a more aerodynamic sitting position.

When consumers in many countries started buying Japanese motorcycles, Harley-Davidson faced a crisis, which led to its purchase by the AMF engine factory in 1969. This ownership change did not improve things, and it looked as if the Harley-Davidson factory might have to shut down. Harley-Davidson's chief designer,

Willie G. Davidson (grandson of one of the founders), decided to buy back the factory in 1981, using capital from some investors.

In an exhibition catalogue published on the occasion of Harley-Davidson's 100th anniversary, there is a description of how Harley-Davidson copied Harley bikers when it developed the Sturgis FXB Shovelhead motorcycle around 1980: "The idea for this bike came from Harley-Davidson's chief designer Willie G. Davidson, after attending the famous Sturgis Rally in South Dakota. He made sketches of the customized bikes he had seen at the rally, and then worked with Harley-Davidson's engineer, Eric Buell, to create the bike."

From the mid-1980s on, Harley-Davidson focused on traditional motorcycles but added many new technical features. In a joint venture with Porsche, Harley introduced a new V2 engine with the name Evolution. At the end of the 1980s, Harleys were owned by an increasingly diverse group of people, far removed from traditional bikers. Wealthy businessmen had begun riding Harleys. You could see them in some of the most fashionable holiday spots in Europe, such as on the French Rivera. Traditional bikers nicknamed this new crowd "Rubbers," short for Rich Urban Bikers. This new market segment prompted Harley-Davidson to introduce more sporty motorcycles. The most popular model for this segment, the Softail, was introduced in the year 2000 with a new 88B engine that makes the motorcycle very comfortable to ride. Harley-Davidson also began manufacturing models targeted at women.

At the end of the twentieth century, Harleys were more in demand in the United States than ever before and were expanding into foreign markets, becoming one of the world's best-known brands. On the list of the world's Most Valuable Brands (in market value), compiled by Interbrand/*BusinessWeek*, Harley-Davidson was number 48 in 2001 and number 46 in 2002. With the focus on innovative new design, the trendsetters once again paid attention to Harley-Davidson. Again continuous product development and innovation played a key role in a category.

APPLE'S IPOD

Apple's iPod MP3 player was conceived at Apple's global headquarters in Cupertino, California, and designed there by British designer Jonathan Ive, who had also designed the iMac, the Apple computer that had made trendsetters want to bring their computers into their living rooms because of its ovoid form and translucent colors.

The iPod was introduced in the autumn of 2001, first in the United States and a month later in Europe. While the very first MP3 players, which were introduced in the late 1990s, looked the way consumer audio electronic products were expected to look at the time—not exactly simple and elegant—the iPod was innovative in several ways: it was a quarter the size of comparable MP3 players, it had an extremely logical user interface, and it had a remarkable design, slim, understated, and white—incandescent. When I first saw it, I thought Prada, the trendy Italian lifestyle brand, could have designed it. Almost all audio equipment at the time was gray or black. Even the iPod earphones were refreshingly white. The introductory price was about $400. By the end of the year, more than 125,000 iPods had been sold.

The iPod was created in a very short time. The engineer in charge of developing it was hired in February 2001 and was told to have the new MP3 player ready for sale in the stores by Christmas of the same year. The briefing was that it should be "simple to use. And gorgeous."

Shortly after its introduction, which included a huge advertising campaign, there was a quick upgrade cycle that increased the number of songs that could be stored on the iPod, and at the same time the price came down. In addition, Apple licensed hundreds of thousands of songs in preparation for its iTunes Music Store.

In the summer of 2002 Apple opened a new store in New York City's then trendy-going-on-mainstream SoHo district, where the majority of stores sell fashion or lifestyle products. As *Newsweek* pointed out, it was the place where Giorgio Armani and the Keith Haring shop coexist. It was Apple's thirty-second retail store, and it was an indication that future stores would be placed in similar locations. At the same time, Apple introduced a new second-generation iPod with a touch-sensitive scroll wheel (a function similar to a touch pad).

In late 2002, Apple announced it would introduce special-edition iPods with the signatures of famous people engraved on the back. You could choose the signature of Madonna, Tony Hawk, Beck, or the NoDoubt logo on the chrome back. It was also possible to have your own design engraved. By the end of that year, 700,000 iPods had been sold. The third generation, which had a different button layout, was announced. At this time the iTunes Music Store opened for online commercial distribution of songs.

By September 2003, Apple had sold 1.4 million iPods, and by the end of 2003 almost 2 million had been sold, giving Apple control of a third of the entire MP3 player market. The following year, a smaller version, iPod Mini, was introduced. It was a completely new design with a scrolling wheel that took up less space and a burnished metallic surface that gave it a futuristic look and feel. It was introduced in five new colors, completely in tune with the fashion industry, which was also having a "color party." Apple also announced that it would create an HP-branded version of the iPod that would be sold with HP products. Museums such as the Mori Art Museum in Tokyo replaced their traditional audio tour guides with iPods. Automaker BMW included a special iPod interface in all its new cars.

By August 2004, when the iPod was featured on the cover of *Newsweek* along with Apple CEO Steve Jobs, more than 3 million iPods had been sold worldwide. That cover showed a photo of the fourth-generation iPod, which had the same scroll wheel as the iPod Mini. The iPod Photo was released in November. Apple also introduced a special U2 edition of the iPod, in black with a red scroll wheel. The U2 version was bundled with a digital boxed set of music by the rock band, and the group did its very first endorsement. During the Christmas 2004 season, 733,000 iPods were sold world-wide, bringing the cumulative total to more than 10 million by year's end. There were more than 100 Apple stores, most of them designed in the style of an upscale fashion store.

In early 2005 Apple introduced the iPod Shuffle, the smallest iPod MP3 player, in all white—still a big contrast to the other small-size MP3 players. Later in the year, Apple introduced the iPod Nano, the thinnest in the iPod series; it was pencil-thin with many innovative features, including album art in the display. The last financial quarter of 2005 was the best Apple had ever had.

In an article about Apple, *Fortune* talked about fusing "fashion, technology, and reverence for personal creativity into something that [Apple CEO Steve] Jobs likes to call the 'Apple user experience.'" The magazine made another reference to fashion, noting that the fun, jellybean-colored iMac introduced in 1998 had quickly became a fashion statement.

A whole new industry of third-party iPod accessories ranging from external speakers to microphones emerged. American accessory designer Kate Spade introduced iPod Mini cases in colors matching the five original iPod Mini colors. Prada, Dior, Gucci, Marc Jacobs, Louis Vuitton, Paul Smith, and Burberry also made cases for iPods. The iPod had become a bona fide lifestyle accessory.

At the beginning of the twenty-first century, Apple had mostly been thought of as a "cult brand" with a limited but loyal following. Financially, the company had had its ups and downs, and just before the iPod was introduced it was downish. The constant reinvention of the iPod meant that the trendsetters had their focus on the product for a much longer time than would have been the case if the iPod had been introduced in just one version. By 2007 Apple had sold 100,000,000 iPods.

This dissection of real-life trends does not include everything that has happened in the trend process. Much more has been going on than has been described in this chapter. But the point is that we can see that there are identical patterns in the trend processes described. It is also worth paying attention to the fact that many of the trend-spotting clues identified in the previous chapters have been at work also in these cases.

The movement of a trend through the Diamond-Shaped Trend Model may look chaotic or haphazard, but it is not. There is a pattern at work, and it was more or less the same at the beginning of the twentieth century as it is at the beginning of the twenty-first century. Only the speed of the process has changed. At the beginning of the twenty-first century, this process—like many other processes—happens a lot more quickly than it did at the beginning of the twentieth century, as the iPod music phenomenon has demonstrated.

All four examples show us that for the trend process to move beyond the trendsetters, the interest of the trendsetters has to be maintained, not only by enough trendsetters, but also for a certain period of time. The observing process is something that takes time, often a longer period of time than one would expect. So to keep the trendsetters interested in the new, innovative style long enough to allow trend followers to observe it, "the pot has to keep boiling" for some time. The main factor in keeping the pot boiling is a continuous development of the style, design, or product. That will also keep the trendsetting media—and other media—focused on the trend. Without this continuous development, the new, innovative style, design, or product is likely to be only a fad.

TO BE OR NOT TO BE OBSERVED

It is important to know all the patterns of a trend if you want to be able to predict future needs, but it is equally important to be aware that the key element in the trend process is about people being observed and observing, often from a distance or through the media.

To sum up: trendsetters start a trend by adopting something that a trend creator has developed. At certain intervals, trendsetters want something that is different from what others are wearing or using. They do not need to see other people actually wearing or using the product (but of course they do need to see the product).

Trends are about style and taste (and the behavior surrounding style and taste), which are things that can be observed. When Gloria Vanderbilt was a teenager, she was observed by two friends, Oona O'Neill [later Mrs. Charles (Charlie) Chaplin] and Carol Marcus (later Mrs. Walther Matthau). Carol Matthau writes in her autobiography about Gloria Vanderbilt: "She was more sophisticated than Oona and I. . . . We tried to redesign ourselves to look like Gloria. We even darkened our eyebrows." She also writes about how they were influenced by the media: "We did each other's hair in styles we saw in those [movie] magazines. . . . Hair down to shoulders like Veronica Lake's, a movie star of the day."

Observing other people that they can relate to is one of the most important ways people adopt new styles. When the market research company Yankelovich asked consumers how they got their knowledge of new styles, more than half answered that they observed what other people were wearing.

Though we may all look at many different kinds of people, we are certainly not inspired by all of them. Mainstreamers may look at trendsetters, but this does not make them change their style.

Research from the University of Bath in England and the University of St. Gallen in Switzerland has documented that people do not observe or get inspiration from just anybody. "They like to make sure their [style] is fashionable and trendy among people who resemble themselves," to quote Professor Brett Martin from the University of Bath, who conducted the research with Swiss colleagues. As the research also showed, not everybody watches or cares about what trendsetting celebrities like David Beckham, Penelope Cruz, Brad Pitt, or Scarlett Johansson are wearing or doing. Most people are more influenced by an endorsement from an "ordinary" person like themselves, according to the research. The findings apply to both men and women.

One case about observing and imitating other people's behavior has been documented by *BusinessWeek*. In 1999, the trendsetter DJ Jill Tracey from Miami, Florida, bought a brand new yellow Ford Focus. She parked it in the parking lot near the hip-hop radio station WEDR 99, where she worked. Engineer Joe Regner, then 21, saw the car in the parking lot. Regner was so intrigued that he stopped, got out of his car, and photographed Tracey's car. He decided to buy a Ford Focus SVT for himself. His girlfriend, Eli Domingues, was about to buy a new car—and after some time she ended up choosing a Focus ZX3.

When the trendsetters adopt a trend, there is a typical pattern. First the trend followers observe the new style and adopt it. Then there are more people for the early mainstreamers to observe, and they end up adopting the style, too. Then there are even more people for the mainstreamers, who are the next trend group to adopt the style, to observe.

In music, there are many examples showing that mainstreamers are not directly inspired by the trendsetters. This was the case with Brazilian funk, a music style originally created by young people in the slums of Rio de Janeiro. These Brazilian trend creators and trendsetters were too far outside mainstream American or European consumers' frame of reference for them to find it cool. Mainstreamers identify with new trends that have been sanctioned by trend followers in accessible and familiar venues.

When Brazilian funk found its way to clubs in Paris and New York City, trendsetters first heard the music played by trendsetting DJs. When trend-following DJs go to the trendsetting clubs, they go back to their own clubs and play the same music for trend followers. If enough trend followers adopt the music, then it is likely that the trend will reach mainstreamers in the same way. When trendsetting DJs from other cities visit the clubs in Paris or New York City, they will take the new music style home with them. In this way, a new music style spreads from city to city, and from country to country.

TREND-SPOTTING CLUES

When we want to spot new and emerging trends, we can learn from the trend characteristics discussed in this chapter:

- A continuous product development must take place so that trendsetters can continuously focus on new aspects of the style, design, or product.
- After some period of time, trendsetters will stop being interested in the original innovative style; this typically happens when new versions of the style or product are presented to the market.
- As soon as trendsetters lose interest in a trendsetting product, new versions of the style or product must be available in order to regain the trendsetters' interest and keep the trend process going. This keeps the trend process active and lets other trend groups become part of the trend process.
- Media with trendsetter appeal must sanction the new product(s) or the new style for it to become a trend.
- The association of celebrities with trendsetter appeal will have a strong influence on a trend.
- Hollywood movies—and movies in general—will have a very strong influence on a trend.

6

TOWARD THE
CLIMAX

IDENTIFYING THE
FINAL CLUES

9 723456 485247

The main feature in the story of a trend is, naturally, whether or not there will actually be a trend. As we have seen, it is the trend-setters who get to decide what will become trends. But this does not mean that everything the trendsetters adopt will become a trend. In many cases, what they adopt will become a fad or maybe not even a fad, just a ripple. Also not all new products, designs, or style innovations will become fad or trends. The reasons for this are multiple.

First of all there is such an overproduction of new styles and tastes today that even the most ardent of trendsetters cannot absorb all of them. Secondly, some innovations are just too extreme to find a market, even among trendsetters. A new kind of clothing may be uncomfortable (like latex clothing). It may even be illegal (like the 1964 topless bathing suit by American designer Rudi Gernreich). It may be difficult to mass-produce (like slacks made of aluminum mesh by American designer Giorgio Sant'Angelo). A style may be culturally too extreme; David Bowie's makeup in the 1970s was too extreme for men. The product may be too expensive for even for very wealthy consumers (for instance, space travel). And if, for whatever reason, it cannot be copied, this can prevent it from becoming a trend.

It is also worth being aware that there are many more fads than trends. This is possible because trendsetters are not clones of one another. They dress differently, but always in innovative new styles, and each product, design, or style can end up being a fad.

And in principle, a seasonal fashion fad never reaches the mainstream; if it did, it would be a trend. In this story, there is a climax only if there is a trend.

So when trying to determine a trend's breakout potential, it is advisable to look critically at the communicable possibilities of what the trendsetters have adopted. Is it easy to observe? Can it be copied or imitated easily? Are different kinds of media spreading the news? If the answer to all these questions is yes, then a new style, sound, or taste is likely to go mainstream. The part about being observable goes hand in hand with one of the clues identified in Chapter 1: a change in style that is the complete opposite of an existing style is more likely to become a trend. For instance, when men's hairstyles go from long hair to a crew cuts, this is very observable—and extremely easy to imitate. In a biography of the late designer and entrepreneur Laura Ashley, one woman who lived in the same area as Ashley in the early 1960s said: "I was very influenced by Mrs. Ashley's peasantry sort of style and tried to do my hair in the same sort of way; in fact, lots of people [in the area] copied her."

What exactly appeals to the trendsetters and what they will adopt will, of course, vary from time to time. But in this investigation, we have already gathered several clues to what sets the action in motion. To sum up, some important clues are that trendsetters often focus on the following:

- Styles and tastes that are completely new and have never been seen before
- Styles and tastes that are outside the mainstream
- Styles or products that are in continuous style development
- Something that has *not* yet been overhyped by the media as a trend

The trendsetters may pick up on something that has just been brought into being by a trend creator, something that has been a trend before (often called retro style), something that has existed for a long time as part of an underground subculture (such as drag queens or bodybuilders), or something that has existed in only one of the trendsetting groups, such as a youth culture, wealthy people, or gay men.

When a change *is* a trend, not just a fad, it will rarely affect the entire population, as pointed out in Chapter 3. The reason for this is simple: not all styles are relevant to all people. Some trends are specific to women, others to men. For example, if we are thinking about hairstyle trends, the kind of hair you have will influence the hairstyle trends in which you are personally interested. If you are a trendsetter and you are bald, it is not likely that you will have a great personal interest in new hair trends (although you may have a professional interest). If we are talking about gardening trends, your interest will depend on your having a garden or an interest in gardening. Some people do not like or are not interested in certain specific types of food and beverage, and therefore changes in taste in these specific types of food and beverage will not affect them.

The reality is that not all individuals with the personality profile of a certain trend group need to adopt a style for it to spread in the Diamond-Shaped Trend Model. When a trend appeals to only a few individuals in each trend group, the trend does not spread quickly. It will often take longer to reach mainstreamers because there will be a longer period of time before mainstreamers feel secure that the trend followers have sanctioned the trend. If many people adopt the trend, there are more people to observe, and mainstreamers can get comfortable with the trend more quickly. A trend group simply does not adopt a trend before that trend group is psychologically ready to adopt it. And the trend process is about the process of adopting the style, not the process of seeing or hearing about the style or taste.

THOSE WHO BUY: THE TREND CONSUMERS

Being a trendsetter is about adopting new style and taste without other people having sanctioned them. How this adoption takes place will vary, but it will often involve some kind of shopping, though there are also changes in style and taste that do not necessarily involve buying something. Growing your hair long does not involve a commercial transaction, and if an untanned body is the trend, you just have to stay out of the sun.

But generally shopping does play an important part in a trend process. And trendsetters do buy products in new styles more often than other consumers. Madonna, the archetypical trendsetter (who is also rich and famous), has said in an interview with *Elle*, "I don't like to look back. Who wants to wear last year's clothes? There are so many new things to buy."

Also soccer player David Beckham has said that he was an avid clothes shopper even before he became rich and famous. When he moved to Manchester to begin his soccer career, he took with him seven bags of clothing; the family he was moving in with had never seen anyone with that much clothing. When he was 22 years old, he was asked by the *Sunday Times* in London when he shopped. His answer: "Monday, Tuesday, Wednesday, Thursday, Friday, and Sunday." (On Saturdays he plays matches.) He also told the newspaper that he is keenly interested in the most trendsetting fashion brands. He said that as a teenager and soccer trainee, he would save his money so that he could buy trendy clothing.

The frequent shopping behavior was confirmed in the surveys done in connection with the development of the Diamond-Shaped Trend Model. In the surveys, the test subjects were asked to state how often they bought new products in three categories: clothing, shoes, and sunglasses. In all three categories, it was evident that the trendsetters bought new products much more often than the conservatives. The trendsetters were the trend group with the biggest consumption of style products in terms of volume.

When we measure the trend groups' buying frequency for clothing and accessories, the consumption pattern appears as a V shape in the Diamond-Shaped Trend Model, indicating that consumption is not relatively the same for the six trend groups. This is illustrated in Figure 6.1. The illustration shows that trend-setters buy new style products more often than conservatives. The different trend groups in the upper half of the Diamond-Shaped Trend Model consume more lifestyle products because of their greater desire for change. This explains why there is room for the many brands with appeal to trendsetters that exist in the market today.

The V shape of consumption also explains the many fads in the market each season. As a matter of principle, most of the seasonal fashion fads do not have a market beyond the trendsetters. This is illustrated in Figure 6.2. Fads come and go quickly. As a sales manager of a European chain of jewelry stores has said: "In a period we sold a lot of wooden jewelry but that [fad] died suddenly one Saturday morning." This is what happens when something new—in this case a certain style of jewelry design—does not get enough momentum in the market to become a trend.

THE SPEED OF THE TREND PROCESS

The Diamond-Shaped Trend Model can be used to analyze a market at any given time. Vertically, it has a time dimension that can be used to track the speed with which different people or consumers adopt a new style and/or taste. When you know the typical speed, you can predict how long it will take for a trend to reach, for example, mainstreamers.

When discussing trends, it is important to be aware that the speed of the process varies depending on the size of the country. The spread of a trend is probably faster in smaller, fairly homogeneous countries than it is in larger, heterogeneous countries.

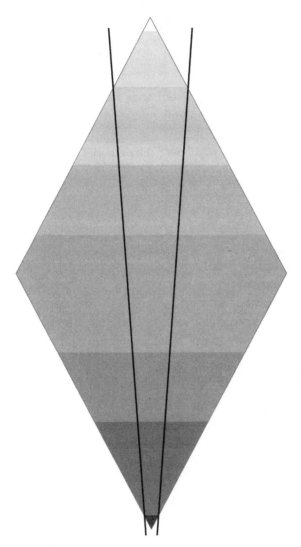

Figure 6.1 The V-shaped consumption pattern in the Diamond-Shaped Trend Model

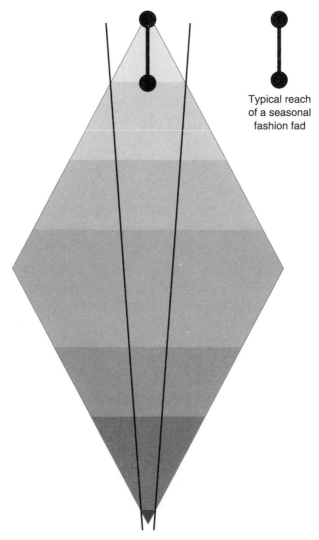

Typical reach
of a seasonal
fashion fad

Figure 6.2 Typical reach of a seasonal fashion fad

We know from studies that small groups or organizations are generally easier to change than large ones. Therefore, changes are likely to be faster in a small European country such as Denmark than in a larger country such as the United States.

The cases presented here come from different countries. For instance, the clothing category case is from Great Britain: in Chapter 2, we saw that the bohemian (boho) style in women's wear was emerging in 1996, documented by *Elle*, among other magazines. It took 10 years before the same magazine said on its cover: "Bye-bye Boho!" There were many different fads in women's fashion during these 10 years, but when design historians document this period in time, they will undoubtedly focus on the boho style.

While we cannot use the cases in this book to give estimates for any one country, maybe we can learn something else. For instance, does the trend process take the same time in different product categories?

Since observing and imitating are such important elements of the trend process, it seems obvious that this process will be faster if a new style or design is easily observable. For instance, cosmetics, hairstyles, and clothing are much more observable than home furnishings and sports equipment, so they should be the fastest.

We can test this theory by summing up some of the cases in this book. First we can estimate how long it takes for a trend to go from the trendsetters to the mainstream (the case studies do not include the time it takes for a trend to be created by a trend creator and gain momentum within the trendsetter group). My estimates of the speed for five different product categories are these:

- Cosmetics: 1–2 years[1]
- Clothes: 2–3 years[2]

1. As men do not use cosmetics in Western culture, this process is different from processes that affect both sexes. Therefore, the speed is faster than for other trends.
2. Based in part on the gray to floral pattern case study in Chapter 3.

- Accessories: 2–3 years[3]
- Home design: 5–7 years
- Sports equipment: 6–8 years

My estimates, based on case studies, for how long it takes for a trend to spread from the top of the Diamond-Shaped Trend Model (the trend followers) to the bottom (late mainstreamers) in the same five product categories are these:

- Cosmetics: 3–5 years[4]
- Clothes: 7–10 years[5]
- Accessories: 7–10 years
- Home design: 12–18 years[6]
- Sports equipment: 15–20 years[7]

From studying trend processes for different product categories, it becomes apparent that the speed of the trend process varies for different product categories, and that something that is very visible and observable moves through the Diamond-Shaped Trend Model more quickly. This can also explain why music is a very fast category, and why changes in food take a long time to go mainstream. The example in Chapter 1 involving cranberries could indicate that changes in food require about 25 years. Music is everywhere—on the radio, on television, in movies, in stores, and on the Internet. We often cannot avoid being exposed to new music, so this may be one of the fastest categories, especially with distribution through the Internet.

3. Based in part on the shoe case studies in Chapter 4.
4. Based in part on the mehndi case in Chapter 2. See note 1 above.
5. Based in part on the case of the bohemian style mentioned in Chapter 2 and elsewhere.
6. Based in part on the minimalist style case in Chapter 1.
7. Based in part on the discussion of inline skates in Chapter 5.

The trend process is faster in the upper half of the Diamond-Shaped Trend Model than in the lower half. This makes sense because we know that the trend groups in the bottom half are more reluctant to change.

Another important lesson to be learned by studying the speed of the trend process in different product categories is that the process is generally faster in lower-priced categories, probably because consumers can afford to buy products in these categories more often. This has also been confirmed by one of Europe's big multibrand chains of fashion and accessories. "The style changes faster for accessories than for fashion," the sales manager of the company's Pieces accessories stores has said to a Danish newspaper. Jewelry and accessories in this chain cost less per piece than clothing.

TRENDY MAINSTREAM?

The trend process begins with the trendsetters and continues to the mainstreamers. When it reaches the mainstream, the trend has peaked. But when is the trend most trendy—when it is the preferred style of the trendsetters, or when it is peaking among mainstreamers? Different people will have different opinions, and a person's point of view on this question is very much dependent upon where in the market that person is focusing: when the trend is emerging or when it has volume.

If you are a small, innovative company or store, it may be very important for you to know what the trendsetters are doing and to focus on them. As soon as they move on to something else, the trend shifts, in your view. But the trend will continue and will perhaps attract the attention of a major company or a big chain of retail stores. These businesses may not pay attention to the trend until the small company or store has been focusing on it for some time. In both instances, we are talking about what is trendy. Some will focus on the emerging trend; others on the peaking trend.

It is when interest in a particular trend diminishes that the style or taste stops being a trend. It does not make sense to talk of something being trendy when the trend is diminishing, even though it is still going through the process of change.

The Diamond-Shaped Trend Model can be useful when discussing trends. Having the model makes it a lot easier to avoid misunderstandings about a new trend. One analyst may be focusing on the style and taste of the trendsetters and another on the style and taste of the mainstreamer, and both can be right. This can be illustrated by looking at popular holiday destinations from multiple points of view.

In 2005, the magazine *Travel & Leisure* published its annual list of the world's best holiday destinations, including the most popular cities to visit. Sydney topped the list for the fifth time. The Top 10 Overall list named the following cities:

1. Sydney, Australia
2. Bangkok, Thailand
3. Rome, Italy
4. Florence, Italy
5. Chiang Mai, Thailand
6. New York City, U.S.A.
7. Istanbul, Turkey
8. Cape Town, South Africa
9. Oaxaca, Mexico
10. San Francisco, U.S.A.

But are these the most trendy travel destinations? Not if you ask a trendsetter like Tyler Brûlé, the founder of *Wallpaper* magazine and *Monocle* magazine. In one magazine interview, he mentioned Buenos Aires, New Zealand, and the Patagonia region in southern Argentina as trendy holiday destinations. These three destinations are also on a Top 10 list of the most trendy travel destinations in 2005 that was compiled by asking 30 Europeans who belong to one or more of the trendsetter groups identified in Chapter 2. They were asked where they had traveled lately or were planning on traveling. This Top 10 list included no European or North American destinations:

1. New Zealand
2. Argentina
3. Australia
4. Cambodia
5. Costa Rica
6. Burma
7. South Africa
8. Chile
9. Morocco
10. Antarctica

Both lists are highly subjective. The first is a reader survey by a popular American magazine with a well-to-do, mostly American readership. The second was compiled from a small, select group of European trendsetters. So which of the lists represents what is trendy—the list covering destinations for trendsetters or the list with very popular (or mainstream) destinations?

If you are looking for new trends in the travel market, it is the latter list that is interesting; those are the places the industry should watch to see if tourism is growing. To the travel industry, there is nothing new in the list of the most popular destinations, but these destinations represent a big market, and to some large travel agencies they may represent what is popular—what they might call trendy.

BUBBLING UP AND TRICKLING DOWN

Since the beginning of the twentieth century, sociologists and social thinkers have been studying how new ideas and knowledge (and to a lesser degree style) are adopted. One of the first theories that they came up with about how style was adopted was the "trickle-down" principle, the assumption that in a society with a social hierarchy, new style innovations start with the upper class and then trickle down to the poorer classes. U.S. social critic Thorstein Veblen and French sociologist Gabriel Tarde were among the proponents of this theory in the early 1900s. They described how wealthy people who could afford to buy new clothing designs were the first to do so. The working class—the majority of people—could not afford to buy these clothes, but these people looked up to wealthy people and aspired to adopt their style innovations. In pre–World War II society, that was the way many changes in style and taste came about.

However, in present-day society, the social and economic relationships among people have changed radically. In the trend process today, the trickle-down principle is not the only way new styles become popular. There is also a "bubbling-up" process, with many examples of changes in style and taste coming from outcasts, poor people, and underground subcultures. Today, trends emerge from all strata of society—even teenage boys and young men from the slums of Rio de Janeiro, with music (as mentioned in Chapter 5) and in footwear. "Up until 1993 Havaianas was a commodity—it was a poor people's shoe. Then it became a fashion accessory," the manager of Brazil's largest and now world-famous manufacturer of flip-flops has pointed out.

This book is about the trend process, and all kinds of people can be involved in a trend process. The entire population is rarely involved in *all* trend processes, but people from all social and economic backgrounds can be part of the trend process. This is because trends are about something that relates to all human beings. In Chapter 1, we defined trends as changes in style and taste. Now we can refine this definition: trends are changes in the following:

- What we can see and read (for instance, design and art, literature)
- What we can taste (for instance, food and drink)
- What we can smell (for instance, fragrance)
- What we can hear (for instance, music, language)
- What we can feel (for instance, dance and travel)

Trends are about things that are observable *outside* of the human body and mind, so to speak—from clothing to cars to food. They are about changes in what we can relate to with our five senses. The idea that trends are about what we can sense lends credibility to the existence of the trendsetter personality. We know from psychology that different people perceive and sense things differently. In learning situations, some people will grasp things better by reading, others will get a better understanding by listening, and still others will learn more quickly by watching something being demonstrated. The fact that some people are more visual in their perception of the world than others will further their interest in everything visual. And if people are more auditory in their perceptions, this will make them more aware of new sounds. The part that these differences can play in the trendsetter personality undoubtedly is extremely complex. It can also explain why people who are trendsetters in fashion are not necessarily trendsetters in music or in food.

NOT JUST ONE FORMULA FOR CHANGE

As pointed out in Chapter 1, there are many different processes for change in society. For instance, there are the fads among children, which is a different process than trends and fads among grown-ups (children are not generally part of a polysocial environment, so for that reason alone it must be a different process, and children are under the influence of grown-ups). It is important to be aware that not all kinds of changes take place in the same way.

Some scientists have been focusing on the way people adopt ideas, technology, and other kinds of knowledge, something that cannot just be observed, at least not in the same way as changes in style and design can be observed. Therefore, it makes sense that ideas and knowledge spread in different ways from style and design changes: ideas and knowledge are *inside* the human mind. The word *trend* may be used as a synonym for changes in values, politics, spirituality, and many other areas, but this does not mean that the process of change is the same as that for changes in style and taste. First of all, people do not generally change their values, political beliefs, or spiritual beliefs as often as they change, say, their wardrobes, and second, the passing on of new ideas and knowledge will often involve some talking, which is not necessary in the trend process (although word of mouth certainly is often part of the trend process).

In the twentieth century, research into how ideas and knowledge spread focused on the personal interaction and communication between individuals. Some scientists have studied how new ideas, new knowledge, and new methods—in farming and birth control, for instance—spread throughout a specific, local population. This is called a diffusion process. (Many people know the term *fusion*, which means "merging or melting together." *Diffusion* means the opposite of fusion, that is, "spreading.")

While many people have studied change processes, there is one scientist who is known for summing up the research on diffusion processes. His name is Everett Rogers, and his best-known book is *Diffusion of Innovations*, which was first published in 1962. This book is specifically about the spread of knowledge concerning technological and scientific advances. The real-life research that

Diffusion of Innovations is based on clearly shows that Rogers was focusing on processes of changes in smaller communities (for instance, the farming community), and not on processes that in principle would affect a large portion of the general population. Therefore, the diffusion process and the trend process could not be more different from each other.

A diffusion process generally takes place within a group that is very similar, for instance, farmers, teachers, or women who are fertile, and the process affects only people who share the particular characteristic. The trend process takes place among people who are very dissimilar, and it affects people who are very different from one another.

A diffusion process takes place in an area of limited geographical scope, typically a smaller or larger community (a village or rural area). The trend process is not limited geographically. In principle, it can affect people all over the world (not necessarily all of them, but some people in all areas of the world).

The diffusion process relies on face-to-face communication, that is, people knowing one another well and talking to one another. People have to know one another and talk to one another for knowledge of technological and scientific advances to spread. In the trend process, people do not have to know one another and they do not have to talk for the trend to spread. This process is about observing other people more than it is about talking to people in one's network, and it is more about mingling than it is about knowing one another.

When the study of diffusion processes took place, the media played a completely different role from the one they play today. In the 1930s, 1940s, and 1950s, when the early diffusion research was carried out, the media did not concern themselves with, say, contraception, and the general media did not write about subjects like farming techniques. There was limited access to knowledge from the media of all kinds. Without a big media influence, the role of opinion leaders—people who voice their knowledge in their social network—is important in a small community.

In the trend process, the media play a big role because what the trend process is about—changes in style and taste in the wider society—is constantly communicated in almost all kinds of media, from Hollywood movies and television sitcoms to print magazines and, in the twenty-first century, also Internet-based media. In the trend process, people do not have to rely on opinion leaders to get news about changes in style and taste.

The early diffusion researchers observed that people adopt new innovations, new knowledge, and new methods at different speeds. One of the first studies involved farmers in Iowa who were presented with a new kind of seed that could increase their harvest by 20 percent. Even with this impressive increase, there were large differences in how quickly the farmers started using the new seed. It took the typical farmer seven years to adopt the new seed. In this and other studies, it was noted that wealthy farmers were quicker than poor farmers to start using the new seed. At the same time, it was noted that the wealthy farmers had a larger social network and were therefore able to tell more people about the new seed.

Based on this and other studies, the so-called Adopter Model was introduced. The Adopter Model classifies people into five categories:

Innovators   Early Adopters   Early Majority   Late Majority   Laggards

The adopter categories have a clear socioeconomic dimension. In this model, the most cosmopolitan, the most well-traveled, the best educated, the most mentally stable, the most empathetic, the most intelligent, the wealthiest, those who believe least in the power of fate, and the most socially active people are found in the Innovators and Early Adopters categories.

Poor people and people without a social network are found in the Late Majority and Laggards categories. In other words, these categories are based on a comprehensive personality profile, having a certain financial status, and having a social network. Only a superficial reflection on the trend groups and adopter categories will show similarities between the two. They are in fact different social phenomena.

In spite of their name, the Innovators in the Adopter Model are not the people who think of new ideas or create new knowledge or develop new methods. They are the first to adopt what *other people* have invented or discovered. Therefore, Innovators are not like trend creators, who are the people who actually create new trends—changes in style and taste.

The socioeconomic profile of most trendsetters is no different from that of other people. A trendsetter does not earn more money or have a better education than someone in another trend group. And it would be wrong to believe that trendsetters are more cosmopolitan than the population in general. Trend creators and trendsetters in many of the world's most trendsetting cities create and adopt new styles just by living in their own neighborhoods. In some cities around the world, trend followers only have to go out into their own streets in order to be exposed to new trends.

There are also differences in how frequently trendsetters and Innovators adopt something new. Trendsetters adopt new styles with a certain regularity. It is doubtful that Innovators adopt new methods and/or new knowledge with the same regularity with which trendsetters consume new styles or new products. It is also doubtful that Innovators adopt more new methods and more new knowledge than people in the other adopter categories end up adopting.

Life has changed dramatically for many people since the studies in diffusion research were carried out. Since the beginning of the 1960s, we have seen a media explosion, not only in paid media, but also in freely accessible media. This has changed the lives of many people in Western societies and even in many other parts of the world. Owning a television set, a radio, or a telephone is something that the majority of people in Western societies can afford—which was not the case in the middle of the twentieth century, when the diffusion process was documented. In addition, information on lifestyle products is communicated to consumers these days whether they watch soap operas, sporting events, or the news.

The huge difference that the media make today can be illustrated by comparing the exposure and publicity surrounding two African American entertainers who achieved worldwide fame a generation apart. In the middle of the twentieth century, Sammy Davis, Jr., was performing all over the United States, tap dancing and singing. As a breather between his tap dancing, he would do what today is known as "moonwalking." This was documented on footage that the singer Michael Jackson later (then in his twenties) would watch when visiting Sammy Davis, Jr., in his Los Angeles home. Moonwalking later became Michael Jackson's signature move after he performed it on a 1983 television special, and it became known all over the world.

OPINION LEADERS

Opinion leader is an important term in diffusion research, and it is closely connected to the Adopter Model. In this model, the Early Adopters are typically the actual opinion leaders, and therefore the opinion leaders have the same characteristics as the Early Adopters. Compared to other people, opinion leaders:

- Read, listen to, or view more media
- Are more cosmopolitan

- Are more social
- Have a larger network
- Have a higher income or greater wealth

Opinion leaders exercise and want to exercise an *active* influence. To be an opinion leader requires a certain personality, one that is more charismatic, charming, extroverted, talkative, eloquent, and knowledgeable than that of the average person. The opinion leader tends to dominate groups of people and/or be the person that many other people want to ask for advice before they do something new or adopt something new. Opinion leaders are found in most kinds of groups and communities—whether the group be a sports association, a trade union, a dinner party, or a company.

In his book *The Tipping Point*, Malcolm Gladwell used the concept of the unusually informed, persuasive, and well-connected opinion leader in explaining how changes take place—all kinds of changes, in fact. But not only is *The Tipping Point* off when using the thinking of opinion leaders to explain how big changes affecting many people can take place in a short time, it is also naïve in thinking that one social theory can explain all kinds of changes that take place in society.

In a critique of *The Tipping Point*, professor of sociology Duncan J. Watts from Columbia University in New York wrote in the *Harvard Business Review*, "The idea is intuitively compelling—we think we see it happening all the time—but it does not explain how ideas actually spread." Even if there are people who are so well connected, computer simulations that Watts and his colleague Peter Dodds have carried out show that what is needed for "the widespread propagation of influence through networks—is the presence not of a few influentials but, rather, of a critical mass of easily influential people, each of whom adopts, say, a look or a brand after being exposed to a single adopting neighbor."

Archetype	Influence	Consumption	Interest	Style or Taste	Reach
Opinion leader	Active, verbal ("recommends")	Does not necessarily own the product or brand	Anything imaginable	Very diverse	Own personal network
Trendsetter	Passive, visual (is observed)	Typically owns the product or brand or adopts the style	New, innovative styles and products	Very homogenous	The trend followers

Figure 6.3 Comparison between opinion leaders and trendsetters

(*Critical mass* is a term from the natural sciences that can, for instance, refer to the number of animals it takes for a species to survive and grow.) Also, we have to be aware that many people who are called opinion leaders by the media are opinion leaders because they are quoted in the media, not because of their personal network of family and friends, and this is something different from an opinion leader in diffusion research.

Figure 6.3 shows a comparison between opinion leaders and trendsetters with respect to their influence, consumption, interest, style or taste, and reach. We now know that the trendsetters are the ones "responsible" for starting the trend process.

TREND-SPOTTING CLUES

When we want to spot new and emerging trends, we can learn from the trend characteristics that have been defined in this chapter:

- Not everything that is new, different, innovative, or called trendy by the media will become or in fact is a trend.
- Sometimes the new may be just too extreme to become a trend, or it will just be a fad.
- Watch what the *majority* of trendsetters are adopting because that is what the other trend groups are most likely to observe.

- Look for clues to a trend across categories that have appeal to different senses (clothing, music, and food, for instance).
- Trendsetters are typically not trendsetters in all categories. Therefore, not everything that a trendsetter does necessarily indicates a new trend.
- The more observable a new style is, the more likely it is to become a trend.
- The more imitable a new style is, the more likely it is to become a trend.

7

ANTICLIMAX

UPS AND DOWNS FOR BUSINESSES

9 723456 485247

rendsetters are very powerful consumers. They have enormous influence on businesses and brands, even big and successful ones, when they sell products that are based on style and taste. The stronger the relationship between a brand and products based on style and taste, the more susceptible the brand is to be under the influence of trends. As we have seen in this book, brands can be around for a long time but only if they change the products they sell. If Harley-Davidson had never changed its products since its founding in 1903, the brand would not have existed 100 years later. Because Levi's did not change its products, the brand lost its once attractive position in the market.

There can be many indicators of a world-famous brand's shifting popularity. One indicator is the brand's position on the Interbrand/*BusinessWeek* Most Valuable Brands list. In 1997, Levi's was number 8 on the list of the world's most valuable brands. In 2001, it was number 67. In 2002, Levi's was number 73, and in 2005, it was number 96. As Levi's moved into the bottom half of the Diamond-Shaped Trend Model, it also slid down in the Most Valuable Brands list.

Many brands and industries have experienced what it means to get—and to lose—the trendsetters as customers. Across industries that have products with appeal to our senses, the influence of the trendsetters has been felt in both small and large companies. One (medium-sized) company was Tommy Hilfiger.

In the 1980s, Tommy Hilfiger was a brand in the classic Ralph Lauren tradition but with lower prices. The Tommy Hilfiger logo was a crest, and the style was inspired by upper-class snobbery. It was exactly these signals that hip-hoppers fell for (as we also saw in Chapter 2) when they began to buy Tommy Hilfiger clothing. From having been a menswear brand, Tommy Hilfiger became a hip-hop brand—and a successful one. But as the hip-hop style became more uniform and lacked continuous renewal, it became less interesting to the trendsetters.

When hip-hop artists no longer also set the agenda in mainstream fashion, it affected Tommy Hilfiger. According to *Forbes Global* magazine, Tommy Hilfiger had to "reorganize" after sales plummeted in 2000: "The same hip-hop crowd that made the clothes famous eventually helped sink the brand, after white suburban kids decided that they'd had enough of the gangster look." That same year, Tommy Hilfiger had to close its flagship store in London.

Tommy Hilfiger could have continued selling hip-hop clothing to the hip-hop segment for many years, as the hip-hop style did not disappear. However, trendsetters no longer found inspiration in the hip-hop culture. That is why the mainstream ended up losing interest in the Tommy Hilfiger brand; they were following new leads of the trendsetters.

A normally trendsetting company's or brand's market position can change quickly if it does not pay attention to the behavior exhibited by trendsetters. But what can be done if a brand that once was trendsetting has slipped to the bottom half of the Diamond-Shaped Trend Model? Just as it is possible to lose customers in the upper of the trend model, it is possible to get their attention again. This is what Burberry, one of England's oldest clothing brands, did very convincingly at the end of the twentieth century.

Burberry is closely linked to the history of the trench coat. Thomas Burberry founded the company in 1856 in Hampshire, and in 1879, he invented a new kind of fabric, which he named gabardine. The fabric was robust and weatherproof. It was later used for the raincoats that the Burberry family began selling around 1900. In the late 1890s, Burberry designed the officer's Tielocken coat, which had a number of functional details. This coat became the forerunner of the trench coat, which got its name because it was worn by officers in the trenches during World War I. In addition to the military, wealthy adventurers and explorers at the beginning of the twentieth century were enthusiastic about the trench coat and other Burberry products. Polar explorers such as Roald Amundsen and R. F. Scott both wore gabardine clothing from Burberry on their expeditions. Also, the pilots of the time used Burberry products and wrote complimentary letters to the company about how happy they were with their clothing.

In 1924, Burberry introduced the beige, black, red, and white tartan pattern that became the company's trademark. In the 1940s, women started wearing its raincoats, though they were considered men's clothing.

In the 1950s and 1960s, a number of movie stars wore Burberry trench coats on the silver screen. Humphrey Bogart and Ingrid Bergman wore them in the movie *Casablanca*, as did Audrey Hepburn in *Breakfast at Tiffany's* and Peter Sellers in the Pink Panther movies. In the 1980s, trench coats were still popular, particularly with yuppies (in England they were called Sloane Rangers), who liked classic brands. But the 1990s brought a problem. The company was still purveyor to the Queen of England and the Prince of Wales—a status symbol that underlined Burberry's reputation as stuffy and old-fashioned, far away from Hollywood glamour. The trench coat and other Burberry clothing mostly appealed to people who were stylishly conservative and certainly did not fit in with the then-new minimalist style or the more "streety" style of the hip-hop artists. Burberry was losing customers.

Something had to be done, and in the summer of 1997, Burberry hired a new CEO, Rose Marie Bravo. At that time, the value of the company was around $353 million. The profit for 1997 was £25 million (compared to £62 million the year before). Bravo began a process aimed at making Burberry trendy and the trench coat fashionable again. The relaunch was to start with both product and marketing innovations. As designing and manufacturing new products is a longer process than coming up with a new marketing plan, the first big task was to produce a new advertising campaign. The creative job went to top-notch photographer Mario Testino and the famous model Stella Tennant, who came from a wealthy, aristocratic English family. The campaign was done in black and white, in contrast to traditional color ads, with a theme of urban modernity interpreted in a British way. The ads were placed only in select trendsetting lifestyle print media.

Bravo then hired the first designers for Burberry's new collections, and in the spring of 1998 she started reducing the number of product licenses. She felt that there were too many of them and that many were of poor quality. The ad campaign for autumn 1998 was shot with a focus on the classic beige tartan and the trench coat.

In the autumn of 1998, Burberry introduced a new upmarket collection named Prorsum. The name is Latin for "forward" and is the Burberry company motto. The collection was shown during London Fashion Week. Colette, then one of Paris's most trendsetting stores, bought the collection. New York's upmarket department store Barneys and the trendy London clothing store chain Joseph did the same. The ad campaign for the following spring was photographed at a motocross rally, with Burberry's PR agency sending out Burberry motocross jackets to British actresses Kate Winslet and Kristin Scott Thomas.

Until this time, the brand name had been Burberrys of London. In the winter of 1998, a new logo was introduced, and Burberrys changed its name to Burberry—without the *s*.

Burberry had its own stores in London, but the locations were wrong. In 1998, the company's management decided to find new locations. Work began on a new flagship store in the fashionable Bond Street district in central London. The Burberry fragrances Burberry and Weekend were relaunched with new packaging and a new ad campaign. Work began on a third fragrance called Burberry Touch.

In the spring of 1999, the Prorsum collection hit the stores. Colette presented the collection in its front windows. The Burberry annual report showed a profit of £11 million. When the campaign for autumn 1999 was going to be shot, Stella Tennant was joined by another top model, Kate Moss—both wearing trench coats.

At the autumn catwalk shows by the international top designers in Paris, Milan, London, and New York, several other designers also presented trench coats in their collections. The trendsetters had begun to buy vintage Burberry trench coats, and several fashion journalists were already wearing trench coats, often the original Burberry trench coat, when they went to see the collections. When Hurricane Floyd hit New York during fashion week, Burberry's U.S. PR agency distributed 30 trench coats to fashion editors as gifts. When *Vogue* editor-in-chief Anna Wintour was photographed wearing a Burberry trench coat, the photo appeared in several New York City newspapers. At the same time, the designers at Burberry began working on a shoe collection.

The business media were picking up on what was happening at Burberry, and Rose Marie Bravo was featured on the cover of *Forbes* magazine. Photos of well-known New Yorkers wearing trench coats were published in the *New York Times*. In her role as Ally McBeal in the popular TV series of the same name, actress Calista Flockhart wore Burberry clothing, as did one of the characters in the popular TV series *Sex and the City*. Photos from that year's *Vanity Fair* Academy Awards party showed British artist Damian Loeb wearing a Burberry kilt. He was described by *Vanity Fair* as the artist most preferred by British trendsetters.

In the next ad campaign, Kate Moss was joined by another aristocrat, Lord Frederick Windsor. When the campaign was published in the spring of 2000, it showed Moss clad in a Burberry bikini. Demand for the new bikini was huge. The profit for 1999 had doubled from the 1998 level—to £21.7 million.

Additionally, the Burberry look, including beige tartans, had been copied in the spring collections of many fast fashion brands. In June 2000, the Burberry summer collection for spring 2001 was reviewed in the *International Herald Tribune* along with many very famous designer brands. In the autumn of that year, the new flagship store on Bond Street opened. Many celebrities attended as guests. The fragrance Burberry Touch was introduced.

In the spring of 2001, Burberry announced its profit for the year 2000: £65.1 million—triple the previous year's profit and the biggest in the company's history.

Also in the spring of 2001, a new female model was introduced in the Burberry ad campaign: Jerry Hall, the former wife of Rolling Stones singer Mick Jagger. In the autumn, a Burberry baby collection was launched. Burberry had more products in its collections than ever before. Its ads were featured in all the major lifestyle magazines, which also started to include Burberry in their coverage of the international catwalk shows. In magazines such as *Elle* and *Vogue*, the models often wore Burberry clothing.

The profit for 2001 was £85.4 million, a new record. In July 2002, Burberry was listed on the London stock exchange. The value of the newly listed company was £1.15 billion. Over the next two years, newspapers reported that sales were better than ever before. In 2005, the value of the company was $3.5 billion.

The trench coat had become a product trend. In 2006, a Danish tabloid newspaper whose readers in general are mainstream to conservative reported that the trench coat was "superhot," and it showed five different trench coats with prices varying from about $80 to $1,000 for the original Burberry trench coat.

At the same time that Burberry was undergoing a transformation, electronics industry giant Samsung was doing the exact same thing and mirroring what was going on at the Burberry head office. Samsung Electronics, founded in South Korea in 1969, was for many years a giant manufacturer of generic electronics—TV sets, radios, and video players, among many other product categories.

Samsung started focusing on design as a key element in product development. The product development teams at Samsung's main manufacturing site also started "exploring ideas and concepts from entirely different industries, picking up hints about the importance of the emotional appeal in the offerings of furniture makers and Hollywood," according to *BusinessWeek*. When Samsung introduced the "world's slimmest 17″ Flat Panel TV," the ads showed a twenty-something woman embracing the TV. The text read: "Dress from Paris. Jewelry from New York. Shoes from Milan. TV from Samsung."

In 1997, Samsung was number 96 on the Interbrand/ *BusinessWeek* Most Valuable Brands list. In 2001, Samsung was number 42, and in 2004 it was number 21. That year, *BusinessWeek* wrote: "No longer known for undercutting the prices of big Japanese brands, the Korean consumer-electronics dynamo is suddenly cool."

The trendsetter dynamic is the same across industries— whether they are about style or taste. If there is nothing to grab the attention of the trendsetters, they move on. And advertising cannot alone keep their attention. It is the innovative products that matters. Without product innovation trendsetters do not pay attention to advertising. This is what the American beer industry found out.

In the 1990s, beer sales were declining. Up to that point, the beer industry as a whole had been hugely successful in industrializing the manufacturing of beer. There was tremendous consolidation. During the twentieth century, an industry that had originally comprised about two thousand independent breweries had been reduced to three major domestic breweries. Together, Anheuser-Busch, Miller Brewing Company, and Coors Brewing Company had 80 percent of the market. This comfortable market also meant that there were few product innovations. As pointed out in Chapter 1, the result was that many consumers stopped drinking beer—just as many people had stopped wearing Levi's when product development had ceased to be prominent at that company. The beer companies relied heavily on advertising, yet fewer people were buying beer.

The industry as a whole did not do anything about this, but there were entrepreneurs who did. One of them was Jim Koch. He had already seen this coming in the 1980s, and as a result he had founded his own brewery, a microbrewery that he called The Boston Beer Company. He had noticed that in New York and other major East Coast cities, there was an interest in imported specialty beer.

The statement that The Boston Beer Company was a microbrewery was quite literal: at first there were only Jim Koch and his secretary-turned-sales manager. The product that the microbrewery launched was called Samuel Adams Boston Lager. Unlike the beers from the large breweries, there was no corn, rice, syrup, sugar, or stabilizers in Samuel Adams Boston Lager. The taste was different, and consumers liked it better than what other breweries had to offer. Samuel Adams Boston Lager went on to win numerous awards and was named "Best Beer in America" at the largest beer festival in the United States. For the first decade of the company's history, it did not advertise.

Almost 20 years later, The Boston Beer Company had become the largest specialty brewer in the United States, and hundreds of microbreweries have been established since Jim Koch founded his company. In 1980, there were only four microbreweries in the United States. In 1997, there were 1,250. Microbreweries also flourished in Europe and South America. In 2000, I visited a microbrewery in Brazil that used coffee beans in the beer-brewing process. With lots of product development, beer had changed its position in the Diamond-Shaped Trend Model—from bottom to top.

HOW OFTEN SHOULD THERE BE A NEW STYLE?

These cases once again stress how important design and product development are if a brand wants to keep its position in the Diamond-Shaped Trend Model. But how often does a brand have to develop a new design in order to keep a desired position in the model? Two examples can show us the consequences of different frequencies of innovative style introductions.

As mentioned in Chapter 1, Prada is one of Italy's traditional leather goods manufacturers. Mario Prada and his brother founded the company in 1913. In 1978 Mario Prada's granddaughter Miuccia Prada took over the company and set about designing the collections. In 1989, Prada launched clothing and shoe product lines. This was the first step in turning Prada into a complete lifestyle concept. Prada quickly became one of the most highly profiled and trendsetting lifestyle brands of the 1990s. The strategy was to introduce brand extensions and open Prada stores all over the world.

According to Miuccia Prada, it was a surprise that the trendsetters were so enthusiastic about her designs. "I focused on doing what I do best and what I enjoy doing, and success just tagged on later . . . I committed myself to making stylish yet functional bags and clothes and harmonizing tradition and innovation," she said in a magazine interview with the eyewear industry magazine *20/20*.

Since 1989, Prada has had one of the most innovative product and design development departments among the major brands in the lifestyle industry. Each season, Prada has presented a new look. This gives fashion journalists something new to write about each season, resulting in numerous articles about Prada products in the trendsetting media.

Expansion and a large number of brand extensions in the 1990s did not cause Prada to lose its appeal to the trendsetters and did not change Prada's position in the Diamond-Shaped Trend Model. Prada was able to keep its position in the Diamond-Shaped Trend Model throughout the 1990s and the first years of the twenty-first century by consistently turning out new, innovative styles, many of which have been widely copied.

Like Prada, Tod's is a brand out of northern Italy, a region rich in craft and design traditions. It was there in 1978 that a cobbler by the name of Diego Della Valle asked Gianni Agnelli, president of the Italian automaker Fiat and the head of a prominent Italian family, if he would like to wear a pair of the company's experimental driving shoes. Agnelli was known as a keen fan of fast cars. Like other drivers, he had sometimes had his shoe slip off the pedal at critical moments when driving. Agnelli liked the shoe, which had soft leather uppers and pebbly rubber soles. The positive feedback inspired the cobbler to establish a shoemaking company, which he named Tod's. The driving shoe became a classic in the shoe business. Actually the shoe's style was—and is—so unusual that it is easy to identify when, for instance, celebrities are wearing them. But, as one fashion magazine reported, it was Agnelli "who catapulted the simple shoes to celebrity status by wearing them with suits and casual wear, while on his yacht or traveling." When Agnelli was photographed by magazines and newspapers wearing Tod's loafers, other prominent Italian businessmen and high society women noticed this. At the same time, the loafer (in its classic form) became an important part of the preppy look of the 1980s. This accelerated the success of the new Tod's shoe, especially in Italy and the United States. Additionally, Princess Diana was seen wearing Tod's. Other famous wearers of Tod's shoes in the 1990s included Princess Caroline of Monaco, Cindy Crawford, Sharon Stone, Catherine Deneuve, Kristin Scott Thomas, Gwyneth Paltrow, Mick Jagger, and Harrison Ford.

By the late 1990s, Tod's shoes were no longer news. Yet, since their look is easily recognizable thanks to the rubber sole that is part of the back of the shoe, Tod's has been able to keep its position in the mainstream market. As *Elle* has commented, Tod's has had an "almost unbelievable lifespan in a world where most designs last a mere season." The explanation—as articulated by Tod's CEO Diego Della Valle to *Elle*—was that, "Every year we . . . tweak the shoe a bit. . . . Add colors or materials, some pastels for spring, for example, but the basic style is the same."

When stilettos became a trendsetting shoe style in 1997, Tod's launched a loafer with a high heel. In 2000, Tod's launched a sportier loafer with a natural-looking rubber sole in a cobranding cooperation with Italian automaker Ferrari. This once again made Tod's a brand that the lifestyle media wanted to report on. *Elle* reported that in the 1990s, sales rose "exponentially." The company went public in 2000, and in the next five years annual sales more than doubled.

The general rule is that the more frequently a brand introduces new style products, the further up in the Diamond-Shaped Trend Model the brand will be positioned. But how often is "frequently"?

In determining how often to develop new products or redesign existing ones to keep a desired position in the Diamond-Shaped Trend Model, we first have to have an understanding of the speed of the trend process in the top half of the model. If, for example, you make sunglasses and you have defined your target group as mainstreamers, you must first find out how long it takes for a new style of sunglasses to spread from trendsetters to mainstreamers.

As an explanatory example we can use the finding from Chapter 6 that it takes about three years for the style of accessories to spread from trendsetters to mainstreamers. This means that if you are a manufacturer of sunglasses and you are targeting mainstreamers, you theoretically have to introduce completely new styles only every third year to avoid being thought of as outdated. If you introduce a new style less frequently than every third year, mainstreamers will begin to feel that your style has become stale. Of course, in order to stay in the market, you have to introduce new products every year, but they do *not* have to be in a completely new style every year.

A sunglasses manufacturer who wants to have trendsetters as its target group can look at the speed of the trend process from trendsetters to trend followers. It is shorter than three years—in my experience, it is about one year in the sunglasses category. A manufacturer who wants to keep the trendsetters as customers must theoretically have sunglasses in a completely new style every year. If the brand introduces new sunglasses styles only every second year, it will have the trend followers as customers instead of the trendsetters.

By working systematically and strategically with trend sociology, companies can have a major influence on their brand's status and life cycle. If management doesn't pay close attention to changes in style and taste, an originally innovative lifestyle brand will inevitably lose its original customers—the trendsetters. They will look for more innovative products from other brands—often new and/or smaller brands. This, in turn, results in these new and smaller brands becoming successful.

A TRENDSETTING INDUSTRY

A long time ago, the fashion industry—as the very first industry—adapted to the behavior of trendsetters, who demand change at certain intervals. Every year, the fashion industry presents new products twice a year. The seasonal product cycles—originally based on changes in the weather—started at the beginning of the twentieth century, when fashion designers started holding biannual presentations of their products. Today, changes in the weather are secondary; now the introduction of new styles as such is more important, and the cycle is based on introducing new products at least every spring/summer and autumn/winter. As other industries began responding to the needs of the trendsetters, they found that their biggest challenge was the constant need for new, innovative styles.

Outside of the fashion industry, one of the first industries to focus on changes in styles on a regular basis was the cosmetics industry. Charles Revson, the founder of Revlon, was in this respect a business trendsetter. He linked his products to what happened in the fashion industry and was enormously successful. As Richard S. Tedlow wrote in the chapter on Revson in his book *Giants of Enterprise*: "Revlon not only advertised extensively by the late 1930s, it also mechanized through packaging, displays, and tie-ins with the fashion themes of the department stores which carried its products. Revson understood early how thoroughly he could promote tie-ups between a magazine, a manufacturer [of women's wear], and key department stores in major American cities." Revson was very focused on introducing new products and creating new fads. And if others created fads, he linked his products to them. This happened in 1945 in connection with the very successful movie *Mrs. Miniver*, which won five Academy Awards. That year, Revlon created the color Mrs. Miniver's Rose, which became hugely successful. Since then, the cosmetics industry has been very focused on associating itself with Hollywood and its stars.

In the twenty-first century, more and more industries are learning from the fashion industry. The sport shoe and sports clothing industries are examples. When sport shoes (sneakers) were first introduced, there were no seasonal product introductions. But today the sport shoe industry has incorporated seasonal changes (although they have little to do with the weather). In the beginning of the 1990s, there were two seasons. But as a representative from Fila has said: "We used to have two seasons, but it's more like four now. We have to recreate ourselves every ninety days with new products in each category—cross-training, running, tennis."

One sport shoe company that has successfully followed the fashion industry model is Puma. In the mid-1900s, there were two dominant sport shoe manufacturers, both German: Adidas and Puma. In the 1960s, Nike became more and more successful, and in the early 1980s, Reebok became successful with its aerobic shoes. By the late 1980s, Nike had become number one in the industry by introducing new, innovative products and gaining celebrity endorsements.

By the early 1990s, Puma was down to a small market share. In 1993, a new CEO took over. According to a European business magazine, he said: "Sell Puma better and more consciously to fewer people." The magazine wrote: "The CEO . . . made the strategic decision of not only to think sport but consciously to identify Puma as a brand that can mix intensive sport with lifestyle and fashion." At Nike, *fashion* was not a popular word. In *The Sneaker Book*, there is a quote by Nike's then director of design: "If you said the word 'fashion' in a Nike meeting, you were really a bad guy. You didn't know what you were talking about."

Puma began a new design strategy that resulted in the company introducing completely new products each season, with new styles in more colors and with more decorative elements, including the creative use of the logo and logo placement. Puma also entered into a partnership with the German fashion designer Jil Sander, and later also with the Japanese designer Yasuhiro Mihara. A model without laces, called Platinum, was launched. As Puma's director of design said in an interview with a Danish business weekly: "It has given us an edge and a different personality from other sport shoe brands. It has been successful, and we have developed the brand in new ways which other brands are now trying to imitate."

According to the same article, this strategy has been a tremendous success. It created double-digit growth rates. Sales of Puma shoes have doubled several times since 1994, and the brand got an image of being cool and trendy. Puma grew 52 percent in 2002 and about the same in 2003.

Sales of both Nike and Adidas shoes in the U.S. market were stagnant during this period, while Puma increased its market share in the United States, Europe, and Japan. Today both Nike and Adidas are thinking along the same lines as Puma, focusing strongly on constant changes in style. Both Adidas and Nike stores have changed dramatically—they now look more like lifestyle stores than like traditional sports clothing stores. And the design and colors of the clothing are changing at regular intervals, which makes the trendsetters buy new sports clothing more frequently.

Also, the car industry is getting inspiration from the fashion industry. In 2002, Patrick LeQuement, head designer at Renault, France's second-largest car manufacturer, told the *Economist* "that ten years ago he would be the only designer attending the Milan fashion show. Now, not only does he send a whole team, but so do other car companies." The magazine also reported that car designers go to architectural shows and graphics exhibitions. "They are out to see what shapes and forms other designers are trying out, and to pick up colours and ideas of their own." Japanese car manufacturers have opened design offices in Los Angeles and London.

Ford Motor Company opened a studio in London's Soho district, "surrounded by video-production houses, strip joints and gay bars," as the *Economist* pointed out. Ford's design office for Lincoln cars moved away from Detroit to Irvine, California.

The results of this association with the fashion world are directly visible in the design of the cars. In the 1990s and early 2000s, nostalgic retro style was popular in fashion and interior design. In the car industry, distinct retro car models like Volkswagen's New Beetle and Kombi, the Mini, Chrysler's PT Cruiser, and the Jaguar XJ were introduced.

INTUITION OR ANALYSIS?

Trends are important to many different people: to the trendsetters, of course, and the many people who like to observe trends, even if they are not trendsetters; to investors, because they can invest in what is going to become a major trend; to businesses, because changes in style and taste play an important role in product development, and because, whether they like it or not, brands are affected by trends. In the twenty-first century, we need to better understand trends because, as the *New York Times* has reported, "Trend-spotting has grown in importance as marketers have become frustrated with some of the traditional tools of market research."

Trend spotting is about getting advance knowledge of what will happen in the market by studying the trendsetters. This can create a competitive edge for businesses because most new product development takes time (in the car industry up to eight years), and the better you can adapt to the market in a short period of time, the more successful you are likely to be. If a business can count on a new trend to grow, it can align its product development with that trend.

As more and more industries become aware of trends, there is a growing need to understand trends better, and there are several kinds of experts with a variety of functions and roles who are ready to give advice. For example, in the 1990s, "cool hunters," as they were dubbed, came on the scene. Cool hunters observe what is going on in the trendy districts of the world's big cities—in the streets, in bars, in restaurants, and in clubs. They seek to answer questions that would be hard to answer from quantitative data: Are young people drinking beer, wine, or cocktails? Which brands do they prefer? What are they wearing? Are they dressing up or dressing down? What kind of music do they listen to?

In the late 1990s, cool hunting got a lot of media attention. But many companies learned the hard way that what the cool hunters reported did not always develop into trends. The *New York Times* reported in an article that "although some cool hunters continue to prowl, the consensus is that their trade has become uncool, because it resulted in no more than a handful of successful products."

One reason for the many miscalculations is that a cool hunter may not know the difference between a new product, a fad, and a trend. In many cases, cool hunters assume that everything that is new is cool and think that it will catch on just because it is new. However, many new products do not stay in the market for long, and about a third of all new product launches end in failure. Of course, this is discovered only after some time has passed, and in that time the cool hunter might be one of the few people who are hooked on the new product.

No doubt there is high value in watching and talking to the trendsetters in their natural habitats, but it is also important to structure the observations and to be able to distinguish between what is a trend and what is a fad, and what will become neither.

If something new is just a fad, it will have a very short life in the market, often such a short life that companies that are not already in on the fad but jump to get in on it arrive just as it is expiring. "By the time clients and creative directors realize that hemlines are going down, they may actually be rising again," as the *New York Times* has pointed out.

Many people use the word *trendy* to refer to both fads and trends, since they both capture the interest of trendsetters. It is not always easy to distinguish between fads and trends, and in principle we only have a chance of knowing whether a change in style or taste will become a trend if we understand the process that creates these changes.

As we have seen, many elements have to come together for a trend to go mainstream. If you want to know very early in the process whether a new change in style and taste will gain momentum and become a trend, the trend-spotting clues outlined at the end of each chapter in this book describe the pattern—or the anatomy—of a trend. The clues are also the key to what sociologists since the 1970s have called a *tipping point* in a process of change, or what natural scientists call critical mass (as mentioned in Chapter 6)—in other words, the signal that a new trend will go mainstream.

The more trend-spotting clues you can identify, the greater the likelihood that a prediction about a change in style and taste will be correct. The 10 most important clues that have to be verified in order to find out whether a trend will gain momentum and spread from trendsetters to the mainstream are the trend-spotting main clues. The more of these clues that are in place at the same time, the greater the likelihood that the trend will become mainstream. The clues do not have to present themselves in a certain order.

This kind of trend spotting involves synthesizing a lot of small signs and observations and seeing if they follow the pattern that characterizes the trend process. A trend analyst uses the main clues to sort the information gained from observing people and systematically monitoring a wide range of media covering lifestyle, design, fashion, fitness, health, beauty, cars, art, travel, interior design, and other fields. Once this information has been collected and sorted, it can be presented with relevant findings, providing others with the opportunity to evaluate its premises, sources, and conclusions.

TREND-SPOTTING MAIN CLUES

A trend is most likely to become mainstream if the following conditions are met:

- The new trend has started as a reaction to what is mainstream.
- Different kinds of trendsetters adopt the trend.
- A high number of trendsetters adopt the trend.
- The trend first emerges in a major city that is known to have many trendsetters.
- The trend quickly spreads to other cities that are known to have many trendsetters.
- There is ongoing product and/or design development early in the trend process.
- The products or style can be imitated or copied.
- Many of the trendsetters' media focus on the trend.
- There is a connection between celebrities and the trend.
- There is a connection between Hollywood movies and the trend.

TREND-SPOTTING CLUES

Companies that want to integrate changes in style and taste into their businesses can learn from the trend characteristics covered in this and the previous chapters:

- You have to develop new products regularly to maintain your position in the market.
- The faster the speed of the trend process in a product category, the more frequently you have to focus on product development in order to maintain your position.
- You get the trendsetters as customers by continuously developing new, highly innovative products, concepts, or styles.

- The more frequently a brand creates innovative products and initiates design development, the higher in the Diamond-Shaped Trend Model the brand will be placed.
- The trendsetters' consumer behavior affects the consumers in the upper half of the Diamond-Shaped Trend Model.
- If you lose the trendsetters as your customers, you also lose the trend followers as customers, and later you will also lose other trend groups. This is how a brand starts spiraling down through the Diamond-Shaped Trend Model.
- Look out for what is going on in the fashion categories. The fashion industry influences the trend creators and trendsetters in many other industries.
- Advertising and other marketing programs influence changes in styles and taste, but it is the actual content of the ad rather than simply the presence of advertising that matters as a clue.
- By understanding the anatomy of a trend, you will have a better chance of spotting and understanding emerging trends and of predicting whether they will go mainstream.

Epilogue

A Continuing Story: The Future of Trends

What does the future hold for trends? Will they change faster? So many things change so quickly in present-day societies that these are very relevant questions to ask.

Predicting the future is much more difficult than predicting new trends. A trend is a process that is driven by human beings in a sociological pattern that has been going on for centuries. The pattern may change sometime in the future, but at present there are no signs of change in the trend process described in this book, except maybe the speed of the process. But predicting the future of trends is as much hit or miss as any other kind of prediction of the future.

However, if we want to try to understand the *near* future of the trend process, we can start by using a historical perspective. This is a commonly used predictive method, and it was the method that physicist Gerald K. O'Neill used in his book *2081* (published in 1981). In *2081*, O'Neill provided this example: In 1781, the world's most advanced mode of transportation was the horse-drawn carriage, which moved at an average speed of 6 miles an hour. In 1881, a train with a steam engine was able to run at an average speed of 60 miles an hour. In 1981, humans were able to travel 600 miles per hour on long-haul commercial flights. On the basis of this development, it is logical for a futurist like O'Neill to predict that in 2081, we will see vehicles moving at a speed of 6,000 miles an hour!

Technology definitely has to be taken into account when discussing the future of trends, and one sure bet is that existing technologies will change in the future. If O'Neill is right about the future of transportation, many things in society will change, and these will also affect trends. However, at the beginning of the twenty-first century there are no signs of such a transportation revolution.

Trends—changes in style and taste—have been going on for hundreds of years. For a long time, concrete trends were slow to emerge, and they stayed current for a long time simply because everything in society was slower (not least transportation and communication) and people were not part of networks the way they are today. In the Middle Ages, populations were much smaller than they are today, and an average person came into contact with fewer people during his or her lifetime than we do today.

Yet there were also changes in style and taste during the Middle Ages. Just one example: although men were generally clean-shaven during that period, chin beards and moustaches came into and out of fashion, as historian Barbara W. Tuchman has reported in her book *A Distant Mirror*. However, the spread of trends took longer then because the fastest mode of land transportation in the Middle Ages was horseback. A person could travel only 30 to 40 miles on an average day's journey riding a horse, and horse-drawn carriages could travel only about 15 to 20 miles a day. Traveling from London, England, to Lyon, France, took 18 days. News got around mostly when aristocrats, artists, and craftsmen traveled. There was a regular postal service between two of the most important merchant cities of the Middle Ages, Venice and Bruges, but it took seven days for a letter to be transported the 700 miles between the two cities.

As transportation, travel, and communications have changed and become much speedier, trends have also begun to last a shorter time. This can be documented by studying the duration of different styles in art, architecture, and decorative arts. Figure E.1 is an overview of the changes in art styles during the period

Name of style	Country of origin	Period[*]	Duration in rounded numbers
Renaissance	Italy	1400-1580	180 years
Baroque	Italy	1580-1730	150 years
Rococo	France	1730-1770	40 years
Neoclassicism	France	1770-1800	30 years
Empire	France	1800-1820	20 years
Romanticism	Northern Europe	1820-1850	30 years
Realism	France	1850-1870	20 years
Impressionism	France	1870-1890	20 years
Expressionism	Northern Europe	1890-1909	20 years
Cubism and early abstract painting	France	1909-1920	10 years
Constructivism and abstract painting	Russia/ Central Europe	1920-1940	20 years
Abstract expressionism	USA	1945-1960	15 years
Pop art	USA	1960-1970	10 years
Conceptual art	USA	1965-1972	7 years

[*]Dates refer to the origin of the style in the country of origin of the style and are approximate. The styles may have different names depending on the genre (art, architecture, or decorative arts) and the country. Some styles are grouped together because they are related. After about 1972, there have been several different styles in art at the same time.

Figure E.1 Changes in art styles since the Renaissance

following the Middle Ages. The Renaissance lasted almost 200 years. As technology improved—for instance, with better horse-drawn carriages—styles and taste changed faster. When the steam-driven train (and later steamships) was invented in the early 1800s, styles and taste changed even faster. With improvements in other kinds of transportation, not least the car, changes in style came about still faster. When commercial jet travel became common in the 1960s, changes in art also happened faster.

In Chapter 2, we saw that the bohemian (boho) style in women's wear was emerging in 1996, as reported in *Elle*. As we saw in Chapter 6, it took 10 years before the same magazine said on its cover: "Bye-bye Boho!" And this was at a time when there had been many changes in electronic communication. But let's have look at what can and will affect the speed of the trend process, and we can start by taking a look at the fashion industry because this industry sets the fastest pace.

For decades, fashion has been sold to stores, either through fashion shows or at fashion fairs, six months before the clothing is going to be sold in the stores. That gives the manufacturers time to produce the clothes that they have sold at the shows or the fairs. There are also clothing manufacturers that own their own stores and can skip selling at fashion fairs. In the United States two well-known examples in this category are chain stores like Gap and Banana Republic. This means that they have six months more to find out which styles they want to sell in their stores.

Nowadays another way to distribute clothing is gaining market share: fast fashion. In this case, manufacturers still sell only through their own stores, but they make a point of getting the newest fashion styles into their stores as quickly as possible. Internationally, Zara and H&M are the two largest fast-fashion chains. Zara, the Spanish chain of clothing stores, can (once fabrics have been bought) deliver newly designed products to its stores in as little as two weeks. As one business magazine wrote: "When Prada presents its newest collection [at a fashion show], Zara has copies in their stores before the Prada originals are in the Prada stores." Zara can do this because some of its manufacturing takes place in Europe, close to most of its stores. This kind of distribution means that trendsetters who are not well-off can get to follow more of the same fads as the well-to-do. But it does not create more fads, because the fads are already there.

A change typically turns into a trend when copying is focused on the other trend groups. The American discount chains Kmart and Target have been in the forefront of "democratizing" design. In the 1980s, Kmart began selling lifestyle products by Martha Stewart. Target joined in some years later, using a simple formula: get a big-name designer to do knockoffs of the same stuff he or she had designed for well-known lifestyle brands. Thus Michael Graves, known for his work for upscale firms like Italy's Alessi, began to supply Target with designs for stainless steel teakettles, blocky wood patio furniture, and plump-handled spatulas. French designer Philippe Starck and fashion designer Isaac Mizrahi have also created products for Target. One consequence is that there will be more people sooner for other consumers to watch and observe, and if there are more people to observe, the trend process will be quicker.

In some industries, the copying happens very fast. As soon as a sketch of a new innovative product has been made by someone who wants to copy, it can be e-mailed to a factory that will make copies. There are many of these in Hong Kong and China. Only rarely is it talked about openly, as when the sales and marketing director of shoe company Majilite told the *New York Times*: "We've had two shoes from Prada . . . copied for the U.S. market."

But copying as such has a long tradition in the clothing industry. As a former assistant to Calvin Klein said of the early 1970s: "Yves Saint Laurent charged two hundred and fifty dollars, and Calvin charged only ten dollars, but the garments were identical."

As copying is so "institutionalized" in the fashion industry, this is not changing the speed of the trend process in clothes.

Copying certainly already goes on in almost all industries. In the auto industry, there are the international motor shows, where the auto manufacturers present new concept cars, which are newly designed cars that are still in development and not in production. Visitors to the car shows in cities like Detroit, Paris, or Tokyo can see the new car models years before they are offered for sale, and so can journalists—very much like in the fashion industry. The other car manufacturers also do not have to wait until the new cars are actually on the market to see what their competitors are doing.

As soon as one car manufacturer has a new type of car, the other manufacturers will follow up on that lead. In the mid-1980s, Renault introduced the first multipurpose vehicle (MPV), the Espace. Today almost all car manufacturers make MPVs. Later Renault introduced the Megane Scenic. According to the *Economist*, "This model sold many times more than forecast and launched a whole new category, known as compact MPVs."

The trend process in the clothing industry cannot go any faster, but if other industries start imitating the fashion industry, we can definitely expect that the trend process in these industries will speed up. This process has already begun in some industries, actually initiated by many of the fashion brands that have started extending their brand names to other categories—to paint (Ralph Lauren), bed linen (Calvin Klein), furniture (Giorgio Armani), and mobile phones (Prada), to name but a few among dozens of examples. With famous brands entering these markets, the established businesses will start looking at what these brands are doing and start developing new styles in order to keep their position in the market. This can speed up the trend process in these industries.

However, if legislation is passed that strengthens copyright laws, especially in design, companies can more easily be fined for copying. This will slow the speed of some design and style trends.

One of the big problems for many brands is counterfeiting. Unlike a copy, a counterfeit, or fake product, is meant to cheat people into believing that it is the original product. A fake product will have the logo and other brand-recognition signs of the original. Almost every kind of industry has problems with counterfeit products today, including electronics, cameras, toys, furniture, and many other products. The quality of the counterfeits may vary, and in some cases it is very easy to see that the product is fake. But often the people buying the products do not care.

Copying and counterfeiting are so widespread that the Counterfeiting Intelligence Bureau at the International Chamber of Commerce estimates that 7 to 9 percent of world trade is in one way or another counterfeited. If there is a crackdown on fake products—if it is made illegal to own fake products—this will slow down the trend process.

For a big part of the twentieth century, most products, from shoes to cameras, were produced domestically. There were both exports and imports, but most Western countries had factories that produced durable goods of almost every kind. With the easing of trade barriers, it became possible to outsource manufacturing to countries with a labor force that was paid much less than in the West. Outsourcing has made many products in the lifestyle categories much cheaper, and this can speed up the trend process in some categories, especially furniture and home furnishings.

Not only goods move more across the globe. People do, too. International travel has been going up and up. There are many reasons for this, including the fact that the real cost of international travel declined by more than 50 percent from 1978 to 2001. With more people traveling this can speed up the trend process.

The media play a big part in the trend process, and as the media change, so can the speed of trends. But not necessarily in the way you would expect.

The many style and lifestyle media channels that are in existence have certainly affected the speed of trends. The lifestyle magazine with the largest circulation is *Cosmopolitan*, which is published in more than 30 languages. With 53 editions worldwide, it has a global readership of more than 60 million each month. So even though we sometimes like to think that the Internet has globalized media, print media actually can also be quite global. And whether we read about something in a printed magazine or on a Web site does not really make much difference; in principle we get the same information.

In daily life, however, it does seem to matter, because readers of Web sites are not necessarily exposed to all the content on the Web sites in the same way readers of magazines normally are exposed to the content contained within their pages. This has to do both with the nature of Web sites (in Web sites we do not browse in the same way that we do in magazines) and with the fact that it is possible to customize news. So if more and more people rely on Web sites and customize the news they get, they may not be as informed about many different aspects of style and taste as they would be by reading printed magazines. This will work against speeding up the trend process. But the Internet certainly makes it possible for trends to spread to many parts of the world faster than they could have in the twentieth century. However, we have to remember that people could actually buy or subscribe to newspapers and magazines in the twentieth century also, and in many cases have them sent almost all over the world, even though this may have taken months. In other words, the Internet has only changed the speed of the process, not the process itself.

The media proliferation has in many ways created an information overload. The media may be available, but they are *not* read, watched, or listened to by all people. More and more people are highly selective in the media that they pay attention to. The result is that not everyone is exposed to the same information at the same time. Not everyone watches the same Hollywood movies, or, for that matter, movies from other parts of the world. This works in slowing down the speed of the trend process.

Not only are people more selective concerning the media they read, watch, and listen to, but the media that they choose to do without are the media that have the potential to influence the most differentiated people at the same time. The existence of polysocial media, that is, media that the polysocial groups read, watch, or listen to, plays an important part in the trend process. In print magazines, *Vanity Fair* and *The New Yorker* are two typical polysocial media, as are many newspapers and news-magazines. As people turn to more and more specialized media, many of the polysocial groups are not exposed to the same information on style and taste at the same time. If designers are reading only media that focus on design and if gay men read mostly gay magazines, this could very well slow down the trend process.

As for the social media—the Web sites that make it easier for people to network—they tend to become more and more specialized, creating smaller and smaller digital communities. A person may join a huge social network like MySpace, but in actual practice a member is not connected to all the people in the network. A person cannot network with more than a few hundred people, max. Most people only have enough time and energy to network with fewer. People may get e-mails, messages, and newsletters very fast and in many different parts of the country in the twenty-first century. But in the twentieth century millions and millions of people would also get the same information at the same time—through television and newspapers with huge circulations. And getting information electronically is not as inspirational to most people as mingling, observing and imitating people in real social settings. And again, reading or hearing about something new is not the same as adopting the new style or taste.

So while most people intuitively would say that the media situation is speeding up the trend process, this may in fact not be the case. For a trend to gain momentum and spread, there must be a lot of attention focused on the new style or taste to get enough people to adopt that style or taste. As the world becomes more individualized, with media to suit individual needs, fewer people will read the *same* media, and this means that a less-varied group of people will get the same information at the same time. And this will make it more difficult for a trend to gain momentum.

The trend process today is the fastest the world has ever seen, but for many reasons it probably will not get much faster anytime soon. We also have to keep in mind that there are more people alive than ever before, and this will have a slowing effect on changes in style and taste, as such changes will take a longer time to affect more people. And because human beings are human beings—not robots—they do not make changes on command, and hundreds of millions of people in the Western world will not make changes in style and taste overnight.

So while some factors are prompting a faster turnover of trends, others are pushing toward a slower turnover. If you are a trendsetter, your style will change often—that is the very nature of being a trendsetter. But there is a limit to how often even trend-setters can change their style—not only for practical reasons, but also because they would lose the advantage of the lifestyle codes. Changing their and taste style too often would make it less effective for them to communicate through their style and taste. They know that one reason for being into new and innovative style is that at least some other people are aware that is what they are.

So for now, the pattern of trends is not likely to change dramatically in the near future. In other words, when you know the anatomy of a trend in the beginning of the twenty-first century, you have a good chance of understanding trends for some time to come.

Acknowledgments

Autobiographies, memoirs, and biographies have been important sources in this book. The subjects of the books certainly were a highly varied group of people, and it was a pleasure to get to know them all. In the future study of the trend process, autobiographies, memoirs, and biographies will be highly valuable, so I would like to thank future writers of these genres in advance.

I have been asked what I consider the greatest invention of all, and I have no doubt about the answer: the written word. Here the original credit goes to the Sumerians, who lived in what is now southeastern Iraq and who started impressing signs on clay tablets about 5,000 years ago. I also want to pay tribute to an inventor who changed the world in a dramatic way: Johannes Gutenberg, the fifteenth-century German who invented book printing in Europe. Without his invention, many trends—for instance, the Renaissance—would not have unfolded in the way that they did.

Jumping to the twenty-first century, I would like to thank my agent, Ed Knappman, who is a true professional and whom it is a privilege to have as an agent. It has also been a great privilege to work with Donya Dickerson, my visionary editor at McGraw-Hill. Thanks also to Jeff Weeks for creating a book cover that made *me* go "wow" when I first saw it.

Trend sociology is still an emerging discipline, but judged solely by the encouragement that I have gotten from students, colleagues, business associates, family, and friends, it may have a future. Thanks to all who have been supportive, both before and after I started writing this book.

Sources

Sources are linked with page numbers and key words from the text in bold, followed by the source(s). As a rule, the few sources that are not in English provide only to factual information. Only in a few cases are observations made personally by the author specified in the sources.

CHAPTER 1

an Old English word meaning "to turn"   6
American Heritage Dictionary (USA: Dell Publishing, 1976).

60 hours   7
Stephen Moore and Julian L. Simon, *It's Getting Better All the Time: 100 Greatest Trends of the Last 100 Years* (USA: Cato Institute, 2000), pp. 98–99.

more leisure time   7
Stephen Moore and Julian L. Simon, *It's Getting Better All the Time: 100 Greatest Trends of the Last 100 Years* (USA: Cato Institute, 2000), pp. 106–107.

8 **Design and Industries Association**
Penny Sparke, *An Introduction to Design and Culture in the Twentieth Century* (England: Allen & Unwin, 1986), pp. 64, 75.

8 **"a sampler of the latest"**
Time (Holland), January 30, 2006.

9 **The term *trendsetter***
Webster's College Dictionary (USA: Random House, 1991).

10 **fortieth anniversary**
www.jfklibrary.org.

10 **book on her style**
Jacqueline Kennedy: The White House Years: Selections from the John F. Kennedy Library and Museum (USA: Metropolitan Museum of Art, 2001).

10 **The following is a chronology**
Textile View (Holland), Spring 2001.
Textile View (Holland), Summer 2001.
Textile View (Holland), Autumn 2001.
Textile View (Holland), Winter 2001.
Textile View (Holland), Spring 2002.
Textile View (Holland), Summer 2002.
Textile View (Holland), Autumn 2002.
Textile View (Holland), Winter 2002.
Textile View (Holland), Spring 2003.
Textile View (Holland), Summer 2003.
Textile View (Holland), Autumn 2003.
Textile View (Holland), Winter 2003.
Textile View (Holland), Spring 2004.
Textile View (Holland), Summer 2004.

"The Vuitton Money Machine," *BusinessWeek* (England), March 22, 2004.

Sixties, Mode d'Emploi (France: Musée de la Mode et du Textile, 2002).

"The School of Cool," *Time* (Holland), February 23, 2004.

"Design in Scandinavia" 12
Berlingske Tidende (Denmark), March 21, 2007.

leather accessories company called Prada 13
Richard Martin, *The St. James Fashion Encyclopedia* (USA: Visible
Ink Press, 1997).

Politikens Modeleksikon (Denmark: Politikens Forlag, 2002).

www.fundinguniverse.com/company-histories/Prada.

"Understated Art" 13
Time (Holland), November 20, 1995.

Giorgio Armani and his American colleague Calvin Klein 13
Steven Gaines and Sharon Churcher, *Obsession: The Lives and Times
of Calvin Klein* (USA: Birch Lane Press, 1994), pp. 199, 341.

In architecture 13
International Herald Tribune (France), June 4, 2007.

Calvin Klein flagship store 13
Herbert Ypma, *London Minimum* (England: Thames & Hudson,
1996).

John Pawson, *Minimum* (England: Phaidon, 1996).

"painted a trendy hotel off-white" 14
Bridget Harrison, *Tabloid Love* (England: Corgi Books, 2007),
p. 147.

Shaker communities 14
June Sprigg and David Larkin, *Shaker* (England: Cassell, 1988),
p. 20.

modernist movement 14
John Pile, *The Dictionary of 20th Century Design* (USA: Da Capo
Press, 1994).

"sent shock waves" 14
International Herald Tribune (France), April 27, 2007.

Women's Wear Daily (USA) April 27, 2007.

14 **"he was always ahead . . ."**
Women's Wear Daily (USA), April 27, 2007.

15 **Paul Rudolph**
Nest (USA), Spring 1999.

www.glbtq.com, the encyclopedia of gay, lesbian, bisexual, trans-gender, and queer culture.

15 **"its clean, uncluttered spaces"**
Jonathan Moor, *Perry Ellis: A Biography* (USA: St. Martin's Press, 1988), p. 42.

15 **happened to be gay**
Jonathan Moor, *Perry Ellis: A Biography* (USA: St. Martin's Press, 1988).

www.glbtq.com, the encyclopedia of gay, lesbian, bisexual, trans-gender, and queer culture.

15 **John Stedila**
Steven Gaines and Sharon Churcher, *Obsession: The Lives and Times of Calvin Klein* (USA: Birch Lane Press, 1994), pp. 111–114.

15 **"the cutting edge"**
Steven Gaines and Sharon Churcher, *Obsession: The Lives and Times of Calvin Klein* (USA: Birch Lane Press, 1994), p. 112.

15 **the late Roy Halston**
Steven Gaines, *Simply Halston: A Scandalous Life* (USA: Jove Books, 1993), p. 128.

15 **Perry Ellis opened his showroom**
Jonathan Moor, *Perry Ellis: A Biography* (USA: St. Martin's Press, 1988), pp. 74–75.

15 **three restaurants**
Tower, Jeremiah: *California Dish* (USA: Free Press, 2003), pp. 118–119.

16 **Memphis design group**
Barbara Radice, *Memphis* (England: Thames & Hudson, 1984).

glamorous clothing   16
Anne Bony, *Les Années 80* (France: Edition du Regard, 1995).

The designers in the Zeus partnership   16
Zeus: *20 Anni di Passione, 1984–2004* (Italy), www.zeusnoto.com.

Alt for Damerne (Denmark), Week 37, 1988.

"Armani Rules," *Newsweek* (England), September 3, 2001.

"Heroes and Icons of the 20th Century" (cover story), *Time* (Holland) June 14, 1999.

Furniture manufacturer Herman Miller   16
www.hermanmiller.com.

Malcolm Gladwell, *Blink* (England: Penguin Books, 2006), pp. 167–172.

"My former home was" (translated from Danish)   18
Borsen (Denmark), June 1, 2007.

"the anti-Rococo trend"   18
H. W. Janson, *History of Art* (USA: Henry N. Abrams, 1995), p. 647.

flipping through books on women's fashion design   18
Charlotte Mankey Calasibetta, *Fairchild's Dictionary of Fashion* (USA: Fairchild Books, 1998).

Richard Martin, *The St. James Fashion Encyclopedia* (USA: Visible Ink Press, 1997).

Colin McDowell, *McDowell's Directory of Twentieth Century Fashion* (England: Frederick Muller, 1987).

Georgina O'Hara, *The Encyclopaedia of Fashion* (England: Thames & Hudson, 1986).

Marie O'Mahony and Sarah E. Braddock, *Sportstech: Revolutionary Fabrics, Fashion & Design* (England: Thames & Hudson, 2002).

John Pile, *The Dictionary of 20th Century Design* (USA: Da Capo Press, 1994).

Politikens Modeleksikon (Denmark: Politikens Forlag, 2002).

Alon Shulman, *The Style Bible: An A-Z of Global Youth Culture* (England: Methuen, 1999).

John Peacock, *The Chronicle of Western Costume* (England: Thames & Hudson, 1991).

John Peacock, *20th Century Fashion* (England: Thames & Hudson, 1993).

Sara G. Forden, *The House of Gucci: A Sensational Story of Murder, Madness, Glamour, and Greed* (England: Perennial, 2001).

Tom Ford: *Tom Ford* (USA: Rizzoli, 2004).

50s Fashion Style (Japan: P-I-E Books, 1997).

19 launch of *Nest*
Nest (USA), Fall 1997.

21 *Megatrends*
John Naisbitt, *Megatrends* (USA: Warner Books, 1988).

John Naisbitt and Patricia Aburdene, *Megatrends 2000* (England: Sidgwick & Jackson, 1990), pp. 53–76.

22 psychologist Abraham Maslow
Abraham Maslow, *Motivation and Personality* (USA: Longman, 1970).

Abraham Maslow, "The Hierarchy of Needs," in Abraham Maslow, *Motivation and Personality* (USA: Longman, 1970), pp. 56, 58.

Abraham Maslow et al., *Toward a Psychology of Being* (USA: Van Nostrand Reinhold, 1968).

Abraham Maslow, *Future Visions: The Unpublished Papers of Abraham Maslow*, ed. Edward Hoffman (USA: Sage Publications, 1996), pp. 3–14.

23 seven needs
David G. Myers, *Psychology* (USA: Worth Publishers, 1998), p. 366.

aesthetic needs   23
Abraham Maslow, "A Theory of Human Motivation," in
Abraham Maslow, *Motivation and Personality* (USA: Longman,
1970), pp. 25–26.

cave paintings   23
H. W. Janson, *History of Art* (USA: Henry N. Abrams, 1995),
pp. 48–57.

when they are well-off   23
Stephen Moore and Julian L. Simon, *It's Getting Better All the
Time: 100 Greatest Trends of the Last 100 Years* (USA: Cato
Institute, 2000), pp. 62–63.

Gallup has asked   24
Gallup News Service, "Wine Gains Momentum as American's
Favorite Adult Beverage" (USA), www.gallup.com, July 18, 2005.

In Germany, beer consumption . . . Great Britain   24
Henrik Vejlgaard, *Trend Management*, 2nd ed. (Denmark:
Borsens Forlag, 2005), pp. 96–97.

"crumbling of the once-dominant"   24
Gallup News Service, "Wine Gains Momentum as American's
Favorite Adult Beverage" (USA), www.gallup.com, July 18, 2005.

a new type of cocktail lounge   25
Vogue (Germany), September 1998.

"Cocktails and martinis"   25
"Cocktails and Martinis Are In," *Elle* (England), 1997.

was the opening of microbreweries   26
Gallup News Service, "Wine Gains Momentum as American's
Favorite Adult Beverage" (USA), www.gallup.com, July 18, 2005.

Boston Beer Company   26
Michael J. Silverstein and Neil Fiske, *Trading Up: The New
American Luxury* (USA: Portfolio, 2003), p. 17.

www.bostonbeer.com.

26 **wine was becoming**
Gallup News Service, "Wine Gains Momentum as American's Favorite Adult Beverage" (USA), www.gallup.com, July 18, 2005.

26 **"Like hemlines and flares"**
Time (Holland), September 12, 2005.

CHAPTER 2

31 *mehndi*
Karl Gröning, *Decorated Skin: A World Survey of Body Art* (England: Thames & Hudson, 1997), pp. 178–179.

31 **Claire Ramsey**
BT (Denmark), February 6, 2000.

31 **"I was traveling"** (translated from Danish)
BT (Denmark), February 6, 2000.

31 **book on street culture**
Janine Lopiano-Midom and Joanne De Luca, *Street Trends* (USA: HarperBusiness, 1997), p. 139.

31 **"a very cool thing"**
National Geographic (USA), August 1999.

32 **"Now it's hugely popular"**
National Geographic (USA), August 1999.

32 **"I often get ideas"** (translated from Danish)
BT (Denmark), February 6, 2000.

32 **"When Julia constructed"**
Aiden Shaw, *My Undoing* (USA: Carroll & Graf, 2006), p. 27.

32 **her DJ Web site**
www.discogs.com/artist/Princess+Julia.

shredded clothing 33
Patricia Morrisroe, *Mapplethorpe: A Biography* (USA: Papermac, 1995), p. 155.

punk movement 33
Ted Polhemus, *Street Style* (England: Thames & Hudson, 1994), pp. 106–108.

"It was a real reaction" 33
Patricia Morrisroe, *Mapplethorpe: A Biography* (USA: Papermac, 1995), pp. 154–155.

"I organized a small" 34
Ralph "Sonny" Barger, *Hell's Angel* (England: Fourth Estate, 2000), p. 21.

Marlon Brando sported the biker look 34
Ephraim Katz, *The Macmillan International Film Encyclopedia* (England: Macmillan, 1996).

dress in the beat style 34
Thomas Powers, *Vietnam: The War at Home* (USA: GK Hall, 1984), p. 202.

long-haired style 34
Ralph "Sonny" Barger, *Hell's Angel* (England: Fourth Estate, 2000), p. 130.

Elizabeth Wilson, *Adorned in Dreams* (England: Virago Press, 1985), p. 202.

Frank Browning, *The Culture of Desire* (USA: Vintage, 1994).

"Looking back" 34
Ralph "Sonny" Barger, *Hell's Angel* (England: Fourth Estate, 2000), p. 72.

The roots of hip-hop 35
Chuck D and Yusuf Jah, *Fight the Power: Rap, Race and Reality* (USA: Delta, 1998).

Russell Simmons, *Life & Def: Sex, Drugs, Money and God* (USA: Three River Press, 2002).

www.zulunation.com.

35 **DJ Kool Herc**
"The Music Portfolio 2005," *Vanity Fair* (England), November 2005.

35 **Grandmaster Flash**
"The Music Portfolio 2005," *Vanity Fair* (England), November 2005.

36 **Sylvia Robinson**
"Hip-Hop Happens," *Vanity Fair* (England), November 2005.

37 **Hip-hoppers aspired**
Ted Polhemus, *Street Style* (England: Thames & Hudson, 1994), pp. 106–108.

Tommy Hilfiger and David A. Keeps, *All American* (USA: Universe Publishing, 1997).

W (USA), September 2001.

37 **"Harajuku girls"**
Fruits (England: Phaidon, 2001).

Fresh Fruits (England: Phaidon, 2005).

37 **Gwen Stefani**
www.gwenstefani.com.

38 **Worth**
Colin McDowell, *McDowell's Directory of Twentieth Century Fashion* (England: Frederick Muller, 1984), pp. 59–60.

39 **a store in New York**
Politikens Modeleksikon (Denmark: Politikens Forlag, 2002), p. 112.

39 **The writer Edmund White**
Edmund White, *My Lives: An Autobiography* (USA: Harper Collins, 2006), p. 73.

Saint Laurent   39
Alice Rawsthorn, *Yves Saint Laurent: A Biography* (England: HarperCollins, 1996), pp. 385–390.

"I like the look"   40
Vogue (England), April 1998.

Hedi Slimane   40
New Yorker (New York), March 20, 2006.

Janet Street-Porter   40
David Beckham, *My World* (England: Hodder & Stoughton, 2000), p. 98.

New Yorker (USA) March 20, 2006.

David Beckham   40
David Beckham, *My Side* (England: CollinsWillow, 2003), photo plates between pp. 308–309.

"no matter how you slice it"   40
Charlie LeDuff, *US Guys* (USA: Penguin Press, 2006), p. 90.

Figure 2.1, chart of trend-creating artists   41
A Guide to Art (England: Little, Brown, 1992).

H. W. Janson, *History of Art* (USA: Henry N. Abrams, 1995).

Benét's Reader's Encyclopedia (USA: HarperCollins, 1987).

John Julius Norwich (ed.), *Oxford Illustrated Encyclopedia of the Arts* (England: Oxford University Press, 1990).

The Reader's Companion to the Twentieth Century Novel (USA: Fourth Estate Publishing, 1994).

Joyce Johnson and Hettie Jones   42
Elizabeth Wilson, *Bohemians: The Glamorous Outcasts* (England: I. B. Tauris, 2000), pp.172ff.

Griswold Lorillard   43
David Grafton, *The Sisters: Babe Mortimer Paley, Betsy Roosevelt Whitney, Minnie Astor Fosburgh: The Lives and Times of the Fabulous Cushing Sisters* (USA: Villard, 1992), pp. 61–62.

43 **tuxedo**
Charlotte Mankey Calasibetta, *Fairchild's Dictionary of Fashion* (USA: Fairchild Books, 1998).

43 **Babe Paley**
David Grafton, *The Sisters: Babe Mortimer Paley, Betsy Roosevelt Whitney, Minnie Astor Fosburgh: The Lives and Times of the Fabulous Cushing Sisters* (USA: Villard, 1992).

43 **"Women in all walks of life"**
David Grafton, *The Sisters: Babe Mortimer Paley, Betsy Roosevelt Whitney, Minnie Astor Fosburgh: The Lives and Times of the Fabulous Cushing Sisters* (USA: Villard, 1992), pp. 85, 152, 153.

44 **Jacqueline Kennedy**
April Witt, "Acquiring Minds," www.washingtonpost.com (USA), December 14, 2003.

44 **Jemima Khan**
Vanity Fair (England), September 2000.

Vogue (U.K.), June 2001.

Elizabeth Wilson, *Bohemians: The Glamorous Outcasts* (England: I. B. Tauris, 2000), p. 232.

Elle (England) September 2005.

44 **"Nearly five years on"**
Brenda Polan, "Is Voyage Now the Most Pretentious Shop in Britain?" *Daily Mail* (England), February 22, 2001.

45 **aesthetically minded**
Article by sexologist and consultant psychiatrist in *I form Magazine* (Denmark), June 1991.

See also John Gray, *Men Are from Mars, Women Are from Venus* (England: Thorsons, 1998), p. 16.

45 **Kinsey Institute**
Heather A. Rupp and Kim Wallen, "Sex differences in viewing sexual stimuli: An eye-tracking study in men and women," *Hormones and Behavior* (USA), no. 51, (2007), pp. 524–533.

"This process has been" 45
"Post-Straight: How Gay Men Are Remodeling Regular Guys,"
Village Voice (USA), August 8–14, 2001.

Absolut vodka 46
"The Buzz on Buzz," *Harvard Business Review* (USA), November-
December 2000.

Katherine Sender, *"Business, not Politics": Gays, Lesbians, Bisexuals,
Transgender People and the Consumer Sphere* (USA: GLAAD
Center for the Study of Media and Society, 2002).

online bank transactions 46
Advocate (USA), April 10, 2001.

hybrid cars 46
Advocate (USA), December 20, 2005.

gay designers 46
www.glbtq.com, the encyclopedia of gay, lesbian, bisexual, trans-
gender, and queer culture.

"Tattoos—once strictly" 47
Iconoculture (newsletter) (USA), Winter 1992/93.

Tattoos 47
Iconoculture (newsletter) (USA), Winter 1992/93.

Vickie Abrahamson, Mary Meehan, and Larry Samuel, *The Future
Ain't What It Used to Be* (USA: Riverhead Books, 1997),
pp. 32–33.

Micha Ramakers, *Dirty Pictures* (USA: St. Martin's Press, 2000).

Terisa Green, *The Tattoo Encyclopaedia* (USA: Simon & Schuster,
2003), pp. x–xi.

Ralph "Sonny" Barger, *Hell's Angel* (England: Fourth Estate,
2000), p. 72.

www.vanishingtattoo.com.

In his autobiography 47
Wakefield Poole, *Dirty Poole: The Autobiography of a Gay Porn
Pioneer* (USA: Alyson Publications, 2000), pp. 183–184.

47 **almost mainstream phenomenon**
www.nationalgeographic.org.

Esquire (USA), March 2002.

www.harrisinteractive.com.

47 **sixth fastest-growing venture**
"A Hole in the Head?" *U.S. News & World Report* (USA), November 3, 1997.

49 **"Amber . . . styled her hair"**
Rich Merrit, *Secrets of a Gay Marine Pornstar* (USA: Kensington Books, 2005), p. 78.

49 **Among Madonna's many**
Madonna, Steve Meisel, and Glenn O'Brien, *Sex* (USA: Warner Books, 1992).

Vanity Fair (England), March 2006.

www.madonna.com.

www.iconmadonna.com.

Elle (England), September 2001.

W (USA), August 2001.

Vogue (USA), July 2002.

49 **"What am I doing"**
Time Style & Design (Holland), Fall 2003.

50 **Bodybuilding was a fringe activity**
George Butler and Charles Gaines, *Pumping Iron* (USA: Fireside, 1973).

Harrison G. Poe, Katharine A. Philips, and Roberto Olivardia, *The Adonis Complex* (USA: Free Press, 2000).

Sam Fussell, *Muscle* (USA: Poseidon Press, 2001).

50 **"American gays"**
Edmund White, *My Lives* (USA: Ecco, 2006), p. 179.

around 13 percent of adult Americans   50
Economist (England), December 21, 2002.

"voguing," a stylized dance   50
Attitude (England), September 2005.

Paris Is Burning (DVD) (USA: Buena Vista Home Video, 2005).

www.madonna.com.

www.iconmadonna.com.

Tim Lawrence, *Love Saves the Day: A History of American Dance Music Culture, 1970–1979* (USA: Duke University Press, 2003), pp. 46–47.

"A hundred food journalists"   51
Jeremiah Tower, *California Dish: What I Saw (and Cooked) at the American Culinary Revolution* (USA: Free Press, 2003), p. 6.

"I've always had"   53
Advocate (USA), March 27, 2007.

"the A group, the wealthy"   54
Esther Newton, *Cherry Grove, Fire Island* (USA: Beacon Press, 1993), p. 266.

In a biography of fashion designer   54
Steven Gaines and Sharon Churcher, *Obsession. The Lives and Times of Calvin Klein* (USA: Birch Lane Press, 1994), p. 156.

In one instance   54
Patricia Morrisroe, *Mapplethorpe: A Biography* (USA: Papermac, 1995), pp. 240–241.

gay fashion designer   54
Patricia Morrisroe, *Mapplethorpe: A Biography* (USA: Papermac, 1995), p. 105.

"Max's was the exact place"   54
Andy Warhol and Pat Hackett, *POPism: The Warhol Sixties* (USA: Harvest Books, 1990), p. 186.

55 **playground**
Charles Kaiser, *The Gay Metropolis* (USA: Harcourt Brace, 1997), pp. 253–259.

55 **Hedi Slimane, who is friends**
New Yorker (USA), March 20, 2006.

55 **friends of Elton John**
David Beckham, *My World* (England: Hodder & Stoughton, 2000), pp. 98, 111.

CHAPTER 3

60 **"I'm a naturally curious person"**
Madonna interviewed by Petra Markgreen Wangler for Swedish Broadcasting Corporation, www.svt.se, Autumn 2005.

60 **"When I was growing up"**
Madonna interviewed by Petra Markgreen Wangler for Swedish Broadcasting Corporation, www.svt.se, Autumn 2005.

61 **Madonna has herself been a chameleon**
www.madonna.com.

www.iconmadonna.com.

61 **Adrianne Philips was the stylist**
Elle (England), September 2001.

W (USA), August 2001.

Vogue (USA), July 2002.

61 **"The most important thing"**
Vogue (USA), July 2002.

62 **"She's quite fearless"**
Elle (England), April 2007.

62 **soccer player David Beckham**
David Beckham, *My World* (England: Hodder & Stoughton, 2000).

including *Time* magazine   62
"Heroes & Icons," *Time* (Holland), April 19, 2003.

his mother is quoted   62
David Beckham—His Life in Words and Pictures (England: Planet
Publishing, 2002), p. 90.

"He has this incredible"   62
Time Style & Design (Holland), Fall 2005.

Diamond-Shaped Trend Model   63
A more detailed documentation of the surveys can be found in
Henrik Vejlgaard, *Trend Management*, 2nd ed. (Denmark:
Borsens Forlag, 2005).

Amish   65
John A. Hostetler, *Amish Society* (USA: Johns Hopkins
University Press, 1993).

I developed this model   65
Henrik Vejlgaard, *Trend Management*, 2nd ed. (Denmark:
Borsens Forlag, 2005), pp. 112–130.

"In the fall of 1998"   66
New York Times (USA), March 21, 2000.

Big Five Personality Factors   69
David G. Myers, *Psychology* (USA: Worth Publishers, 1998),
pp. 432–433.

Abraham Maslow   70
Abraham Maslow, "The Hierarchy of Needs," in Abraham Maslow,
Motivation and Personality (USA: Longman, 1970), p. 58.

In one survey   70
A more detailed documentation of the surveys can be found in
Vejlgaard, *Trend Management*, 2nd ed.

75 **5 percent can be characterized as trendsetters**
- Number of artists: 2001 Current Population Survey, www.cpanda.org.
- U.S. 2000 census count: www.census.gov.
- Annual incomes: Household Income 1999, Census 2000 Brief, www.census.gov.

Number of gays: Glenn Wilson and Qazi Rahman, *Born Gay: The Psychobiology of Sex Orientation* (England: Peter Owen, 2005), pp. 13–27.

Advocate (USA), April 24, 2001.

Advocate (USA), December 19, 2000.

76 **a number of studies**
David G. Myers, *Psychology* (USA: Worth Publishers, 1998), pp. 143–145.

76 **Paul Costa and Robert McCrae**
R. R. McCrae and P. T. Costa Jr., "Clinical Assessment Can Benefit from Recent Advances in Personality Psychology," *American Psychologist* (USA), vol. 41, 1986, pp. 1001–1003.

76 **"For the great majority"**
R. R. McCrae and P. T. Costa Jr., "Self-Concept and the Stability of Personality: Cross-Emotional Comparisons of Self-Reports and Ratings," *Journal of Personality and Social Psychology* (USA), vol. 43, pp. 1282–1292.

76 **The research has documented**
P. T. Costa Jr. and R. R. McCrae, "'Set Like Plaster?' Evidence for the Stability of Adult Personality," in T. Heatherton and J. Weinberger (eds.), *Can Personality Change?* (USA: American Psychological Association, 1993).

David G. Myers, *Psychology* (USA: Worth Publishers, 1998), p. 144.

78 **"[Visconti] would go"**
Gaia Servadio, *Luchino Visconti: A Biography* (England: Weidenfeld & Nicolson, 1982), p. 48.

"By combing small markets" 78
Gaia Servadio, *Luchino Visconti: A Biography* (England: Weidenfeld & Nicolson, 1982), p. 128.

"It was open house" 79
Gaia Servadio, *Luchino Visconti: A Biography* (England: Weidenfeld & Nicolson, 1982), p. 180.

Louis Vuitton 79
"The Vuitton Money Machine," *BusinessWeek* (European edition), March 22, 2004.

www.vuitton.com.

CHAPTER 4

former GIs and combat pilots 82
Ted Polhemus, *Street Style* (England: Thames & Hudson, 1994), pp. 26–28.

Ralph "Sonny" Barger, *Hell's Angel* (England: Fourth Estate, 2000), pp. 25–31, 50.

Douglas Brode, *The Films of the Fifties* (USA: Carol Publishing, 1992).

surfing also was the epitome 83
Amy de la Haye and Cathie Dingwall, *Surfers, Soulies, Skinheads and Skaters* (England: V&A Publications, 1996).

Ted Polhemus, *Street Style* (England: Thames & Hudson, 1994), pp. 48–49.

www.surfline.com.

Jack London 83
Nat Young, *History of Surfing* (USA: Palm Beach Press, 1996), p. 46.

www.surfline.com.

83 **Duke Kahanamoku**
www.surfingmuseum.org.

84 **Hobie Alter**
Nat Young, *History of Surfing* (USA: Palm Beach Press, 1996), p. 75.

84 **dress code**
Textile View (Holland), Winter 2005.

85 **wardrobe designers**
William Mann, *Behind the Screen: How Gays and Lesbians Shaped Hollywood* (USA: Penguin Books, 2001), p. 227.

85 **set decorators**
William Mann, *Behind the Screen: How Gays and Lesbians Shaped Hollywood* (USA: Penguin Books, 2001), pp. 215–218.

85 **"swept the nation"**
William Mann, *Behind the Screen: How Gays and Lesbians Shaped Hollywood* (USA: Penguin Books, 2001), p. 219.

85 **Sunshine & Noir**
New York Times (USA), November 29, 1998.

85 **"cutting-edge collectors"**
New York Times (USA), November 29, 1998.

85 **world's leading design schools**
Economist (England), December 21, 2002.

85 **when a small group of young writers**
Benét's Reader's Encyclopedia (USA: HarperCollins, 1987).

John Julius Norwich (ed.), *Oxford Illustrated Encyclopedia of the Arts* (England: Oxford University Press, 1990).

The Reader's Companion to the Twentieth Century Novel (USA: Fourth Estate Publishing, 1994).

86 **Herbert Huncke**
Thomas Powers, *Vietnam: The War at Home* (USA: GK Hall, 1984), p. 201.

gay sailors   86
Manuel Castells, *The Power of Identity* (USA: Blackwell
Publishers, 2000), pp. 212–221.

highest concentrations   86
Richard Florida, *The Rise of the Creative Class—and How It's
Transforming Work, Leisure, Community and Everyday Life*
(USA: Basic Books, 2004), p. 22 (preface to the 2nd edition).

"The mutation from"   86
Ted Morgan, *Literary Outlaw: Life and Times of William S.
Burroughs* (USA: Henry Holt, 1986), p. 199.

"In many ways"   87
Listener (New Zealand), October 24, 2006.

"We do lots of demos"   87
Michael J. Silverstein and Neil Fiske, *Trading Up: The New
American Luxury* (USA: Portfolio, 2003), p. 132.

wine awakening   87
Michael J. Silverstein and Neil Fiske, *Trading Up: The New
American Luxury* (USA: Portfolio, 2003), p. 179.

"American revolution"   87
Michael J. Silverstein and Neil Fiske, *Trading Up: The New
American Luxury* (USA: Portfolio, 2003), p. 195.

Herman Miller   88
www.hermanmiller.com.

Malcolm Gladwell, *Blink* (England: Penguin Books, 2006),
pp. 167–172.

Whitney Museum   89
David Grafton, *The Sisters: Babe Mortimer Paley, Betsy Roosevelt
Whitney, Minnie Astor Fosburgh: The Lives and Times of the
Fabulous Cushing Sisters* (USA: Villard, 1992), p. 121.

89 **percentage of gay men**
Richard Florida, *The Rise of the Creative Class—and How It's Transforming Work, Leisure, Community and Everyday Life* (USA: Basic Books, 2004), p. 19 (preface to the 2nd edition).

90 **"One weekend Peter and I"**
Wakefield Poole, *Dirty Poole: The Autobiography of a Gay Porn Pioneer* (USA: Alyson Publications, 2000), p. 149.

90 **police harassment**
Charles Kaiser, *The Gay Metropolis* (USA: Harcourt Brace, 1998), pp. 145–146, 197–202.

90 **first discotheques**
Tim Lawrence, *Love Saves the Day: A History of American Dance Music Culture, 1970–1979* (USA: Duke University Press, 2003), p. 14.

91 **Ice Palace**
Esther Newton, *Cherry Grove, Fire Island* (USA: Beacon Press, 1993), p. 244.

91 **"an electronic genius"**
Esther Newton, *Cherry Grove, Fire Island* (USA: Beacon Press, 1993), p. 244.

91 **"There were people dressed"**
Tim Lawrence, *Love Saves the Day: A History of American Dance Music Culture, 1970–1979* (USA: Duke University Press, 2003), p. 31.

91 **racially mixed**
Tim Lawrence, *Love Saves the Day: A History of American Dance Music Culture, 1970–1979* (USA: Duke University Press, 2003), p. 47.

91 **"We used to dress"**
Tim Lawrence, *Love Saves the Day: A History of American Dance Music Culture, 1970–1979* (USA: Duke University Press, 2003), p. 49.

"The regulars donned"   92
Tim Lawrence, *Love Saves the Day: A History of American Dance
Music Culture, 1970–1979* (USA: Duke University Press, 2003),
p. 78.

"leather bomber jackets"   92
Steven Gaines and Sharon Churcher, *Obsession. The Lives and
Times of Calvin Klein* (USA: Birch Lane Press, 1994), p. 200.

"making a big splash"   92
Tim Lawrence, *Love Saves the Day: A History of American Dance
Music Culture, 1970–1979* (USA: Duke University Press, 2003),
p. 73.

"Every designer"   92
International Herald Tribune (France), December 26, 2006.

artistic center shifted   93
H. W. Janson, *History of Art* (USA: Henry N. Abrams, 1995),
pp 546–617.

American expatriates   93
Elizabeth Wilson, *Bohemians: The Glamorous Outcasts* (England:
I. B. Tauris, 2000), pp. 151ff.

"one morning we who lived"   93
Elizabeth Wilson, *Bohemians: The Glamorous Outcasts* (England:
I. B. Tauris, 2000), p. 227.

was the bikini   94
Patrik Alac, *The Bikini: A Cultural History* (USA: New Line
Books, 2005).

until 1965 you could get a citation   94
Meredith Hall, *Without a Map* (USA: Beacon Press, 2007),
pp. 5–7.

Paris was to fashion   94
Alice Rawsthorn, *Yves Saint Laurent: A Biography* (England:
HarperCollins, 1996).

94 **Fragrance**
Richard Stamelman, *Perfume: Joy, Scandal, Sin—A Cultural History of Fragrance from 1750 to the Present* (USA: Rizzoli, 2006).

94 **"No one drank wine"**
Edmund White, *My Lives* (USA: Ecco, 2006), p. 171.

94 **Chuck Williams**
Michael J. Silverstein and Neil Fiske, *Trading Up: The New American Luxury* (USA: Portfolio, 2003), p. 162.

www.williams-sonoma.com.

95 **young French chefs**
International Herald Tribune (France), February 15, 2007.

95 **"There was simply no"**
Robert Mondavi and Paul Chutkow, *Harvests of Joy: How the Good Life Became Great Business* (USA: Harcourt, 1999), p. 22.

95 **especially appealing to those groups**
Elizabeth Wilson, *Bohemians: The Glamorous Outcasts* (England: I. B. Tauris, 2000), p. 145.

95 **homosexual novelist Klaus Mann**
www.glbtq.com, the encyclopedia of gay, lesbian, bisexual, transgender, and queer culture.

95 **"was swarming with foreigners"**
Klaus Mann, *The Turning Point* (England: Oswald Wolff, 1984), p. 119.

96 **it was not until the mods**
Ted Polhemus, *Street Style* (England: Thames & Hudson, 1994), pp. 50–53.

96 **"Swinging London"**
Shawn Levy, *Ready, Steady, Go: Swinging London and the Invention of Cool* (England: Fourth Estate, 2002).

Mary Quant   96
Politikens Modeleksikon (Denmark: Politikens Forlag, 2002),
pp. 248–249.

Together with friends she cut   96
Lynn Darling, *Necessary Sins* (USA: Dial Press, 2007), p. 7.

Working-class mods rebelled   97
Ted Polhemus, *Street Style* (England: Thames & Hudson, 1994),
pp. 69–71.

punk style   97
Ted Polhemus, *Street Style* (England: Thames & Hudson, 1994),
pp. 15, 89–93.

Sloane Rangers   97
Ann York and Peter Barr, *The Official Sloane Ranger Handbook*
(USA: St. Martin's Press, 1983).

10,000 painters and sculptors   97
Elizabeth Wilson, *Bohemians: The Glamorous Outcasts* (England:
I. B. Tauris, 2000), pp. 151ff.

"Let's try"   98
Time (Holland), August 30, 2004.

Author's observations in Milan, Italy, interviewing designers
working in Milan between 1992 and 2000.

"Like most people"   98
Michael J. Silverstein and Neil Fiske, *Trading Up: The New
American Luxury* (USA: Portfolio, 2003), p. xii.

www.victoriassecret.com.

La Perla   98
www.laperla.com.

"a free-floating community"   99
Roberto Verganti, "Innovating through Design," *Harvard
Business Review* (USA), December 2006, p. 116.

100 **Phil Knight**
J. B. Strasser and Laurie Becklund, *Swoosh: The Unauthorized Story of Nike and the Men Who Played There* (USA: HarperBusiness, 1993), pp. 15–21.

100 **Tokyo youth culture**
Fruits (England: Phaidon, 2001).

Berlingske Tidende (Denmark), April 22, 2001.

Vogue (England), September 2000.

100 **"dramatic and enduring influence"**
International Herald Tribune (France), February 26, 2007.

101 **"Very Tokyo."**
Vogue (USA), May 1999.

101 **each district**
Nigel Kendall (ed.), *Time Out Guide to Tokyo* (England: Penguin, 2000).

101 **"Takeshita Dori is a little"**
Scene (England), Summer 2000.

101 **A Bathing Ape**
24 Timer (Denmark), September 7, 2006.

www.bape.com.

101 **"into the U.S. from Tokyo"**
Wall Street Journal (USA), March 29. 2007.

102 **fast food for laborers**
International Herald Tribune (France), June 9–10, 2007.

102 **"When I first tried sushi"**
International Herald Tribune (France), June 9–10, 2007.

102 **"an increasing number"**
Vanity Fair (England), June 2007.

102 **As the magazine also reported**
Vanity Fair (England), June 2007.

In London, sushi   102
Proquest Information and Learning Company, quoted in *Elle*
(England), April 2007.

world's largest metropolitan area   103
Japanese Statistics Bureau, www.stat.go.jp.

areas where artists lived   103
Elizabeth Wilson, *Bohemians: The Glamorous Outcasts* (England:
I. B. Tauris, 2000), pp. 38, 42, 44ff.

"negro actors, lawyers, engineers"   103
Stanley Jackson, *An Indiscreet Guide to Soho* (England: Muse
Arts, 1946), p. 106.

"the only milieu"   104
Edmund White, *My Lives* (USA: Ecco, 2006), p. 280.

Montmartre   104
Elizabeth Wilson, *Bohemians: The Glamorous Outcasts* (England:
I. B. Tauris, 2000), pp. 42–43, 145.

Notting Hill   104
Elizabeth Wilson, *Bohemians: The Glamorous Outcasts* (England:
I. B. Tauris, 2000), p. 233.

East End   104
Elizabeth Wilson, *Bohemians: The Glamorous Outcasts* (England:
I. B. Tauris, 2000), pp. 46ff.

Meatpacking District   104
Vogue (England), November 2000.

Bridget Harrison, *Tabloid Love* (England: Corgi Books, 2007),
p. 170.

"Fueled by the recent"   104
W (USA), September 2001.

cultural power centers   105
Jacques Attali, *Millennium: Winners and Losers in the Coming
World Order* (USA: Times Books, 1991), p. 27.

106 **Tattoos were originally**
Terisa Green, *The Tattoo Encyclopaedia* (USA: Simon & Schuster, 2003), pp. x–xi.

106 **Captain James Cook**
Chambers Biographical Dictionary (England: Chambers, 1984).

107 **flight connections**
www.airlineroutemaps.com.

109 **sudden rise in sales figures**
Malcolm Gladwell, *The Tipping Point* (USA: Little, Brown, 2000), pp. 3–5.

109 **Hush Puppies have been produced**
www.hushpuppies.com.

"The Buzz on Buzz," *Harvard Business Review* (USA), November-December 2000.

Charlotte Mankey Calasibetta, *Fairchild's Dictionary of Fashion* (USA: Fairchild Books, 1998).

Winslow Farrell, *How Hits Happen* (USA: HarperBusiness, 1998), pp. 38, 67.

Linda O'Keefe, *Shoes* (USA: Workman Publishing, 1996), pp. 266–267.

Alon Shulman, *The Style Bible* (England: Methuen, 1999), p. 122.

Jane (USA), November-December 1997.

Unzipped (DVD) (USA: Miramax, 1995).

110 **shown on American television; Sundance Film Festival**
www.imbd.com.

110 **Mizrahi is openly gay**
Unzipped (DVD) (USA: Miramax, 1995).

www.imbd.com.

110 **Jeffrey Miller**
Vogue (England), Autumn 1999.

Bartlett (who is gay) 110
Washington Post (USA), June 2, 1998.

Hush Puppies sales figures 111
Malcolm Gladwell, *The Tipping Point* (USA: Little, Brown, 2000), pp. 3–5.

1998 book 111
Winslow Farrell, *How Hits Happen* (USA: HarperCollins Business, 1998), p. 130.

Birkenstock is the name of 112
www.narcisorodriguez.com.

www.birkenstock.com.

"A Brave New Face for Milan Designers," *International Herald Tribune* (France), March 3, 1998.

Ted Polhemus, *Street Style* (England: Thames & Hudson, 1994).

Ted Polhemus, *Stylesurfing* (England. Thames & Hudson, 1994).

Emanuel Rosen, *The Anatomy of Buzz* (USA: HarperCollins Business, 2000), pp. 64, 69, 228, 255.

Harpers & Queen (England), September 2005.

Women's Wear Daily (USA), May 7, 2007.

"I combine them" (translated from Danish) 113
Eurowoman (Denmark), April 2000.

"queues around the block" 113
Guardian (England), August 29, 2003.

Uggs boots is both a generic term 114
Guardian (England), August 29, 2003.

USA Today (USA), December 10, 2003.

Sydney Morning Herald (Australia), March 13, 2004.

New Zealand Herald (New Zealand), January 19, 2006.

www.deckers.com.

www.uggaustralia.com.

115 **Lucy Benzecry**
Guardian (England), August 29, 2003.

115 **celebrities**
Guardian (England), August 29, 2003.

CHAPTER 5

120 **"disco music was heard"**
Newsweek (England), April 30, 1979.

121 **The origin of blue jeans**
Irga Wintzell, *Jeans och Jeanskultur* (Sweden: Nordiska Museet, 1985).

William Gilchrist and Roberto Manzotti, *Cult—Visual History of Jeanswear* (Switzerland: Sportswear, 1992).

Tommy Hilfiger and David A. Keeps, *All American* (USA: Universe Publishing, 1997).

Janine Lopiano-Midom and Joanne De Luca, *Street Trends* (USA: HarperBusiness, 1997), p. 55.

Douglas Brode, *The Films of the Fifties* (USA: Citadel Press, 1992).

123 **dude ranches**
M. Jean Greenlaw, *Ranch Dressing: The Story of Western Wear* (USA: Lodestar, 1993), p. 43.

123 **singing cowboys**
Ted Polhemus, *Street Style* (England: Thames & Hudson, 1994), p. 23.

Holly George-Warren and Michelle Freedman, *How the West Was Worn: A History of Western Wear* (USA: Harry N. Abrams, 2001), pp. 72–85.

124 **in Sweden**
Irga Wintzell, *Jeans och Jeanskultur* (Sweden: Nordiska Museet, 1985).

"Their clothes are strange" 125
Meredith Hall, *Without a Map* (USA: Beacon Press, 2007), p. 33.

"blue jeans change everything." 125
Lynn Darling, *Necessary Sins* (USA: Dial Press, 2007), p. 7.

Patti Smith 125
Patricia Morrisroe, *Mapplethorpe: A Biography* (USA: Papermac, 1995), p. 155.

hypermasculine look 125
Elizabeth Wilson, *Adorned in Dreams* (England: Virago Press, 1985), p. 202.

Hal Fischer, *Gay Semiotics* (USA: NFS Press, 1977).

Angelo from New York City 126
Irga Wintzell, *Jeans och Jeanskultur* (Sweden: Nordiska Museet, 1985).

Gloria Vanderbilt 126
Steven Gaines and Sharon Churcher, *Obsession. The Lives and Times of Calvin Klein* (USA: Birch Lane Press, 1994), p. 214.

"the jeans exploded" 126
Steven Gaines and Sharon Churcher, *Obsession. The Lives and Times of Calvin Klein* (USA: Birch Lane Press, 1994), p. 215.

20 percent share of the market 126
Steven Gaines and Sharon Churcher, *Obsession. The Lives and Times of Calvin Klein* (USA: Birch Lane Press, 1994), p. 250.

Levi's faced a serious crisis 127
Berlingske Tidende (Denmark), February 26, 2006.

"Although initially Evisu" 128
www.evisu.com.

"It was the first" 128
Vogue (USA), September 2001.

128 **Gucci launched blue jeans**
Tom Ford, *Tom Ford* (USA: Rizzoli, 2004).

129 **"a . . . trendy array of people"**
Bridget Harrison, *Tabloid Love* (England: Corgi Books, 2007),
p. 125.

129 **treatment techniques**
Jeans + Casuals Insider ABC (Germany: Langenfeld, 2000).

130 **"Designer denim is"**
Vogue (USA), September 2001.

130 **In 2005**
Time Style & Design (Holland), Summer 2005.

130 **Levi's introduced**
www.levis.com.

Vanity Fair (England), May 2007.

130 **In the 1990s, inline skating**
Robert Crego, *Sports and Games of the 18th and 19th Centuries*
(USA: Greenwood Press, 2002), p. 80.

www.rollerblade.com.

131 **Venice Beach**
Eyewitness Travel Guides, *Los Angeles* (England: Dorling
Kindersley, 1997).

132 **American Sports Data**
www.americansportsdata.com.

Henrik Vejlgaard, *Trend Management*, 2nd ed. (Denmark:
Borsens Forlag, 2005), p. 159.

132 **new product developments in inline skates**
133 new events created the following news stories:
134 Author's observations of editorials and advertising in the following magazines: *Men's Health* (USA), *Men's Fitness* (USA), *Fit for
Fun* (Germany), and *I form* (Denmark), 1990–1998.

Henrik Vejlgaard, *Trend Management*, 2nd ed. (Denmark:
Borsens Forlag, 2005), pp. 160–161.

Sporting Goods Manufacturers Association   134
www.sgma.com.

Sports Tracking Europe   134
www.npdworldwide.com.

www.inlineplanet.com.

introduced by Harley-Davidson   134
William Green, *Harley-Davidson: The Living Legend* (USA:
Crescent Books, 1997).

www.harley-davidson.com.

Hells Angels bikers were famous   135
Ralph "Sonny" Barger, *Hell's Angel* (England: Fourth Estate,
2000), pp. 28–30, 60–63.

Ralph "Sonny" Barger writes   136
Ralph "Sonny" Barger, *Hell's Angel* (England: Fourth Estate,
2000), pp. 62–63.

motorcycle lifestyle in the movies   136
Douglas Brode, *The Films of the Fifties* (USA: Carol Publishing,
1992), pp. 86–87.

"The idea for this"   138
Museum of New Zealand Te Papa Tongarewa, Wellington,
Harley-Davidson 100 Years (New Zealand, 2003) [catalogue].

Most Valuable Brands   138
"The Best Global Brands," *BusinessWeek* (England), August 6, 2001.

"The Top-100 Brands," *BusinessWeek* (England), August 5, 2002.

Nicholas Kochan, *The World's Greatest Brands* (USA: New York
University Press, 1997).

139 **Apple's iPod MP3 player**
140 www.apple.com.
141
142 *Berlingske Tidende* (Denmark), July 23, 2001.

"iPod World," *Newsweek* (Atlantic edition, USA), August 2, 2004.

"Armani, Andy and Apple," *Newsweek* (U.S. edition, USA), July 29, 2002.

"The Zen of Fighting iPod," *Newsweek* (Atlantic edition, USA), March 7, 2005.

Berlingske Tidende (Denmark), January 23, 2006.

139 **"simple to use. And gorgeous."**
"iPod World," *Newsweek* (Atlantic edition, USA), August 2, 2004.

141 **"fashion, technology"**
"How Big Can Apple Get?" (cover story), *Fortune* (Holland), February 21, 2005.

143 **"She was more sophisticated"**
Carol Matthau, *Among the Porcupines: A Memoir* (USA: Orion Books, 1992), pp. 11, 12, 14.

143 **the market research company Yankelovich**
Emanuel Rosen, *The Anatomy of Buzz* (USA: HarperCollins Business, 2000), p. 106.

143 **Research from the University of Bath**
Brett A. S. Martin, Daniel Wentzel, and Torsten Tomczak, "Effects of Susceptibility to Normative Influence and Type of Testimonial on Attitudes toward Print Advertising," *Journal of Advertising* (USA), 2007.

143 **"They like to make sure"**
Press release from the University of Bath, England, www.bath.ac.uk/news/releases, February 2007.

144 **Ford Focus**
"Buzz Marketing" (cover story), *BusinessWeek* (England), July 30, 2001.

Brazilian funk   144
"Sex and Drugs Are Set to Music in Brazil's Exploding Funk Scene," *International Herald Tribune* (France), July 12, 2001.

CHAPTER 6

Rudi Gernreich   148
Peggy Moffit and William Claxton, *Rudi Gernreich Book* (USA: Rizzoli, 1991).

slacks . . . by American designer Giorgio Sant'Angelo   148
Steven Gaines and Sharon Churcher, *Obsession: The Lives and Times of Calvin Klein* (USA: Birch Lane Press, 1994), p. 176.

"I was very influenced"   149
Anne Sebba, *Laura Ashley: A Life by Design* (England: Weidenfeld & Nicolson, 1990), p. 55.

"I don't like to look back."   151
Elle (England), April 2007.

"Monday, Tuesday, Wednesday"   151
David Beckham—His Life in Words and Pictures (England: Planet Publishing, 2002), p. 90.

This was confirmed in the surveys   151
The surveys are described in more detail in Henrik Vejlgaard, *Trend Management*, 2nd ed. (Denmark: Borsens Forlag, 2005), pp. 128–130.

"In a period" (translated from Danish)   152
Berlingske Tidende (Denmark), February 12, 2006.

smaller, fairly homogeneous countries   152
Winslow Farrell, *How Hits Happen* (USA: HarperCollins Business, 1998), p. 69.

155 **organizations are generally easier**
Henry Mintzberg, *Structures in Fives: Designing Effective Organizations* (USA: Prentice-Hall, 1983), pp. 123–128.

155 **"Bye-bye Boho!"**
Elle (England), September 2005.

157 **"The style changes faster"** (translated from Danish)
Berlingske Tidende (Denmark), February 12, 2006.

158 **world's best holiday destinations**
"2005 World's Best Awards" (cover story), *Travel & Leisure* (USA), August 2005.

158 **Tyler Brûlé**
Seasons (Sweden), no. 1, 2006.

158 **asking 30 Europeans**
Informal survey by author.

160 **Thorstein Veblen**
Thorstein Veblen, *The Theory of the Leisure Class* [1899] (USA: Dover Publications, 1994).

160 **Gabriel Tarde**
Gabriel Tarde, *The Laws of Imitation* (USA: Henry Holt and Company, 1903).

160 **"Up until 1993 Havaianas"**
Monocle (England), June 2007.

161 **people perceive and sense things differently**
David G. Myers, *Psychology* (USA: Worth Publishers, 1998), pp. 146–205.

162 **diffusion process**
Everett M. Rogers, *Diffusion of Innovations* (USA: Free Press, 1995).

164 **farmers in Iowa**
Everett M. Rogers, *Diffusion of Innovations* (USA: Free Press, 1995), pp. 31–35.

documented on footage   166
Vanity Fair (England), March 2007.

singer Michael Jackson   166
Michael Jackson, *Moon Walk* (USA: Doubleday, 1988).

the role of opinion leaders   166
Everett M. Rogers, *Diffusion of Innovations* (USA: Free Press, 1995), p. 27.

The Tipping Point   167
Malcolm Gladwell, *The Tipping Point* (USA: Little, Brown, 2000), pp. 3–5.

"The idea is intuitively"   167
Duncan J. Watts, *Harvard Business Review* (USA), February 2007.

"the widespread propagation"   167
Duncan J. Watts, *Harvard Business Review* (USA), February 2007.

critical mass   167
Philip Ball, *Critical Mass: How One Thing Leads to Another* (England: Arrow Books, 2004).

CHAPTER 7

shifting popularity   172
"The Best Global Brands," *BusinessWeek* (England), August 6, 2001.

"The Top-100 Brands," *BusinessWeek* (England), August 5, 2002.

Nicholas Kochan, *The World's Greatest Brands* (USA: New York University Press, 1997).

"The 100 Top Brands," *BusinessWeek* (England), August 1, 2005.

173 **Tommy Hilfiger**
www.tommyhilfiger.com.

Tommy Hilfiger and David A. Keeps, *All American* (USA: Universe Publishing, 1997).

Richard Martin, *The St. James Fashion Encyclopedia* (USA: Visible Ink Press, 1997).

173 **"The same hip-hop crowd"**
"Cult brands" (cover story), *Forbes Global* (England), 2001.

173 **Burberry**
174 www.burberry.com.
175 *Vogue* (England), Autumn 2000.
176
177 *Vogue* (USA), September 2001.

Richard Martin, *The St. James Fashion Encyclopedia* (USA: Visible Ink Press, 1997).

Colin McDowell, *McDowell's Directory of Twentieth Century Fashion* (England: Frederick Muller, 1984).

Charlotte Mankey Calasibetta, *Fairchild's Dictionary of Fashion* (USA: Fairchild Books, 1998).

Giorgina O'Hara, *The Encyclopedia of Fashion* (England: Thames & Hudson, 1989).

"Hot Summer Trend: IPO Madness," *Time* (Holland), July 8, 2002.

Berlingske Tidende (Denmark), January 13, 2003.

Borsen (Denmark), July 15, 2002.

Time Style & Design (Holland), Fall 2005.

177 **Danish tabloid newspaper**
Ekstra Bladet (Denmark), March 4, 2006.

178 **Samsung**
www.samsung.com.

Nicholas Kochan, *The World's Greatest Brands* (USA: New York University Press, 1997).

"The Best Global Brands," *BusinessWeek* (England), August 6, 2001.

"The Top-100 Brands," *BusinessWeek* (England), August 9, 2004.

"exploring ideas and concepts" 178
"Camp Samsung," *BusinessWeek* (England), June 22, 2006.

"world's slimmest" ad 178
Economist (England), December 21, 2002.

"No longer known" 178
"The Top-100 Brands," *BusinessWeek* (England) August 9, 2004.

In the 1990s, beer sales 179
Gallup News Service, "Wine Gains Momentum as American's Favorite Adult Beverage" (USA), www.gallup.com, July 18, 2005.

Michael Silverstein and Neil Fiske, *Trading Up: The New American Luxury* (USA: Portfolio, 2003), p. 201.

80 percent of the market 179
Michael J. Silverstein and Neil Fiske, *Trading Up: The New American Luxury* (USA: Portfolio, 2003), p. 201.

Boston Beer Company 179
www.bostonbeer.com.

Michael J. Silverstein and Neil Fiske, *Trading Up: The New American Luxury* (USA: Portfolio, 2003), pp. 209–216.

1,250 microbreweries 180
International Herald Tribune (France), December 18, 1997.

Microbreweries also flourished in Europe 180
The Brewers of Europe statistics from 2002, http://stats.brewersofeurope.org.

Prada 180
Richard Martin, *The St. James Fashion Encyclopedia* (USA: Visible Ink Press, 1997).

Colin McDowell, *McDowell's Directory of Twentieth Century Fashion* (England: Frederick Muller, 1984).

"The 100 Top Brands," *BusinessWeek* (England), August 1, 2005.

180 **"I focused on doing"**
20/20 (England), May 2001.

181 **Tod's**
www.todsgroup.com.

Time (Holland), August 30, 2004.

"The Soul of a Luxury Shoe," *Fortune* (USA), July 11, 2005.

"Pedigree Pays for Fay," *Time* (Holland), November 25, 2002.

"Italian Survey," *Wallpaper* (England), November 2002.

181 **"who catapulted"**
Harper's Bazaar (USA), December 1997.

182 **"almost unbelievable"**
Vanessa Friedmann, *Elle* (USA), 1998.

182 **"Every year we"**
Vanessa Friedmann, *Elle* (USA), 1998.

182 **went public**
www.todsgroup.com.

184 **"Revlon not only"**
Richard S. Tedlow, *Giants of Enterprise: Seven Business Innovators and the Empires They Built* (USA: HarperBusiness, 2003), p. 262.

185 **"We used to"**
Tom Vanderbilt, *The Sneaker Book: Anatomy of an Industry and an Icon* (USA: New Press, 1998), pp. 50–51.

185 **Nike had become number one**
J. B. Strasser and Laurie Becklund, *Swoosh: The Unauthorized Story of Nike and the Men Who Played There* (USA: HarperBusiness, 1993).

185 **"Sell Puma better"** (translated from Danish)
Berlingske Tidendes Nyhedsmagasin (Denmark), September 23, 2003.

"The CEO . . . made" (translated from Danish) 185
Berlingske Tidendes Nyhedsmagasin (Denmark), September 23, 2003.

"If you said the word" 185
Tom Vanderbilt, *The Sneaker Book: Anatomy of an Industry and an Icon* (USA: New Press, 1998), p. 130.

Jil Sander 186
www.puma.com.

"It has given us" (translated from Danish) 186
Berlingske Tidendes Nyhedsmagasin (Denmark), September 23, 2003.

double-digit growth 186
Berlingske Tidendes Nyhedsmagasin (Denmark), September 23, 2003.

Sales . . . were stagnant 186
"Puma Sharpens Its Claws," *BusinessWeek* (England), September 16, 2002.

"Jochen Zeitz," *BusinessWeek* (England), July 7, 2003.

more like lifestyle stores 186
BusinessWeek (England), November 3, 2003.

"that ten years ago" 186
Economist (England), December 21, 2002.

"Trend-spotting has grown" 187
"Agencies Look beyond Focus Groups to Spot Trends," *New York Times* (USA), January 2, 2006.

car industry up to eight years 187
"Cool jobs," *Advocate* (USA), July 17, 2007.

"although some cool hunters" 188
"Once Hot, Now Not, Hunters of Cool Are in a Deep Freeze," *New York Times* (USA), July 7, 2002.

188 **a third of all new**
Robert C. Cooper, *Product Leadership* (USA: Perseus Books, 1998), p. 20.

188 **"By the time clients"**
"Agencies Look beyond Focus Groups to Spot Trends," *New York Times* (USA), January 2, 2006.

189 **called a tipping point**
Thomas Schelling, "Dynamic Models of Segregation," *Journal of Mathematical Sociology* (USA), vol. 1, 1971, pp. 143–186.

Thomas Schelling, *Micromotives and Macrobehavior* (USA: W. W. Norton, 1978).

Mark Granovetter, "Threshold Models of Collective Behavior," *American Journal of Sociology* (USA), vol. 83, 1978, pp. 1420–1443.

EPILOGUE

193 **In 1781**
Gerald K. O'Neill, *2081* (England: Jonathan Cape, 1981), p. 33.

194 **beards and moustaches**
Barbara W. Tuchman, *A Distant Mirror: The Calamitous 14th Century* (USA: Penguin Books, 1987), p. 54.

194 **transportation in the Middle Ages**
Barbara W. Tuchman, *A Distant Mirror: The Calamitous 14th Century* (USA: Penguin Books, 1987), pp. 56–57.

195 **Figure E.1, Art historic periods and their duration**
A Guide to Art (England: Little, Brown, 1992).

Dictionary of Art Terms (England: Thames & Hudson, 1995).

Dictionary of Art and Artists (England: Thames & Hudson, 1994).

H. W. Janson, *History of Art* (USA: Harry N. Abrams, 1995), p. 647.

"Bye-bye Boho!"   196
Elle (England), September 2005.

Zara   196
Cecilia Monllor, *Zaratropolis: La Historia Secret de un Imperio de la Moda* (Spain: Ediciones del Bronce, 2001).

Elle (Sweden), April 2004.

H&M   196
Time Style & Design (Holland), Spring 2004.

"When Prada presents" (translated from Danish)   196
Berlingske Tidendes Nyhedsmagasin (Denmark), April 28, 2003.

copying   197
Berlingske Tidende (Denmark), February 8, 2001.

BT (Denmark), April 16, 2001.

Eurowoman (Denmark), April 2000.

Elle (Sweden), April 2004.

Colin McDowell, *McDowell's Directory of Twentieth Century Fashion* (England: Frederick Muller, 1984), pp. 51–58.

Michael J. Silverstein and Neil Fiske: *Trading Up: The New American Luxury* (USA: Portfolio, 2003), pp. 61–62.

Newsweek (England), September 17, 2001.

Time (Holland), May 21, 2001.

Kmart   197
Christopher Byron, *Martha Inc.: The Incredible Story of Martha Stewart Living Omnimedia* (USA: John Wiley & Sons, 2003), pp. 133–154.

Target   197
Roberto Verganti, "Innovating through Design," *Harvard Business Review* (USA), December 2006, pp. 114–122.

www.target.com.

197 **"We've had two shoes"**
"A Walk on the Wild Side Stirs the Shoe Industry," *New York Times* (USA), July 9, 2000.

197 **"Yves Saint Laurent charged"**
Steven Gaines and Sharon Churcher, *Obsession: The Lives and Times of Calvin Klein* (USA: Birch Lane Press, 1994), p. 129.

198 **Renault Espace**
Economist (England), December 21, 2002.

198 **"This model sold"**
Economist (England), December 21, 2002.

198 **strengthens copyright laws**
Women's Wear Daily (USA), April 26, 2007.

199 **counterfeiting**
Economist (England), May 17, 2003.

David Hopkins, Lewis T. Kontnik, and Mark Turnage, *Counterfeiting Exposed: How to Protect Your Brand and Market Share* (USA: John Wiley & Sons, 2003).

Time (Holland), August 23, 2004.

199 **7 to 9 percent**
EC Report on Responses to the EC Green Paper on Counterfeiting and Piracy (Belgium, June 1999).

199 **real cost of international travel**
Michael J. Silverstein and Neil Fiske, *Trading Up: The New American Luxury* (USA: Portfolio, 2003), p. 58.

200 **53 editions worldwide**
www.hearstcorp.com.

201 **through television**
BusinessWeek (England), July 12, 2004.

Index

About the Author

Henrik Vejlgaard, M.A., M.Sc., is a pioneer in trend sociology, the study of the trend process. Combining a background of social science and communication, he consults with a wide cross section of companies and industries on the topics of innovation and product development. He has lectured on lifestyle and trend sociology at the University of Copenhagen and the University of Arhus School of Business, both in Denmark. He has written three books in Danish about consumer behavior, trends, and design strategies. Visit his Web site at www.henrikvejlgaard.com.